The Year of Luke

The Year of

LUKE

Eugene A. LaVerdiere, S.S.S.

Celebration Books

Kansas City, Missouri

Portions of this book previously appeared in
Celebration: A Creative Worship Service.

Library of Congress Catalog Card Number: 79-89487

ISBN: 0-934134-01-4

Illustrations: James Ryon

To Uncle Willy

Grace and peace
for 50 years of priestly service
in the Congregation of the Most Blessed Sacrament

CONTENTS

Preface

Luke-Acts is the work of one man. But his effort gave expression to the searching, sharing and reflection of the community to which he belonged as well as of numerous other communities within his Christian horizon. So also with this book. All who find it useful should join me in thanking the many persons and communities that contributed to it.

I especially want to acknowledge my debt to my family: my parents Gladys and Laurier, my sister Claudette, and my brothers Gary and Peter. My religious family, the Fathers and Brothers of the Most Blessed Sacrament, will recognize here our society's sensitivity to eucharistic values in Christian life and worship. For years, my uncle, William LaVerdiere, S.S.S., has been a gentle, creative critic whose concern reaches beyond the literary and pastoral to the quality of his nephew's religious and apostolic life. This book is dedicated to him on the 50th anniversary of his ordination to the priesthood.

I want to thank also the faculty and administration of the Jesuit School of Theology in Chicago, where I teach in the department of biblical theology. Their warm support and scholarly discussion are reflected in these pages, along with that of many others with whom I have been associated in the Christian quest for biblical understanding and interpretation.

Finally, the editors of *Celebration*—Art Winter, Jerry DuCharme and Bill Freburger—focused my attention on the present enterprise, and generously supported my efforts during the past three years. God must provide editors with a special grace!

To all, my loving gratitude.

Chicago
Corpus Christi, 1979

2

Introduction

Every third year, the church *Lectionary* celebrates the year of Luke. He is a literary minister of the word, whose early Christian history presented gentile churches with a narrative of the events fulfilled in their midst (Luke 1:1-3). His account covers Christianity's first three decades, beginning with what Jesus did and taught (Acts 1:1) and ending with Paul's unhindered preaching at Rome (Acts 28:30-31). In his presentation, these earliest years illumine the challenges of Christian life and mission in the mid '80s of the first century.

Luke provides an important synthesis of Christianity's first half century. He shows us how we too may reflect on our historical origins to understand better the present and its openness to the future. For Luke as for us, this reflection leads us to recognize the reliability of the gospel tradition at a new moment in Christian history (1:4).

Most of the year's readings from Luke's two-volume work, Luke-Acts, are from the first volume, *The Gospel according to Luke*. It furnishes the third or gospel lesson in the Sunday *Lectionary* of cycle C. However, the second volume, *The Acts of the Apostles*, is not slighted. It provides the first reading from Easter to Pentecost Sunday.

A work for our time

Luke-Acts is an especially appropriate work for our time. In their service of the gospel, the Lukan communities had moved beyond their origins and had encountered external resistance and persecution as well as internal difficulties. The community problems emerged especially in the areas of Christian leadership and social equity in communities that included both rich and poor. Shaken by these developments, Christians suffered from Christ's experiential absence and felt a sense of historical discontinuity and uprootedness.

Luke-Acts responded to this Christian identity crisis by reviewing the traditions transmitted by the original eyewitnesses and ministers of the word (Luke 1:2) and by re-reading the prior narrative syntheses of Christian origins (Luke 1:1). The times called for a fresh presentation of events, developed by further reflection on the scriptures and on their interpretation by Jesus' work and teaching.

In this way, Luke gave new vitality to Christianity's deepest impulse. He helped his readers come to terms with the social realities of the greater world in which they were called to a long-term mission of evangelization. His work unfolds as a narrative correlation of promise and fulfillment. Each historical fulfillment constitutes a further promise. He boldly confronts innovative developments and situates them in a series of manifestations of God's creative Spirit. Paul's work is carefully grounded in that of the first apostles, just as theirs is grounded in Jesus' mission. Persecutions reflect the pattern of Jesus' death-resurrection. Internal difficulties are challenged by Jesus' attitude and behavior as well as by the implications of his gospel.

As a whole, the work has a sensitivity to God's presence in everyday human life. We can aptly describe it as a gospel of God's Spirit acting through the humanity of Jesus and his church for the salvation of all. For Jesus and the church, prayer is the experiential context for gospel revelation and for the gift of the Spirit.

Luke's time was a new juncture in Christian history. So is our age which faces the fresh challenge of secular life and institutions. In the process, cherished aspects and institutions of our past have been called into question. Venturing forth with the gospel, we have met resistance. Our Christian commitment has sometimes proven weak and inadequate.

Luke-Acts will not give us a precise response to our situation, since the historical and cultural distance between our time and the late first century is enormous. However, it does point out the way to respond and invites us to review our tradition and to reformulate it according to the scriptures and Jesus' life and word.

Liturgical context

Luke-Acts is a pastoral document aimed at the growth and development of communities dedicated to the Christian mission. The *Lectionary* puts this work in a specifically liturgical context. The setting that gives it ultimate meaning is the actual celebration of the Lord's supper. Accordingly, each reading focuses on one or more aspects of the eucharistic commitment to renew Christ's gift of himself that all might live. The reading is part of an acceptable sacrifice, an act of praise in spirit and in truth in which the risen Lord can be recognized.

The reading from Luke is related to the other readings in the liturgy of the word. The first is usually an Old Testament precedent for the gospel's central theme. It stands as promise in relation to gospel fulfillment and invites the community to reflect on the living gospel according to the scriptures. The psalm after the first reading translates its message into a meditative prayer response to spark our commitment and open us to further revelation. The second reading, frequently from one of Paul's letters, shows us the gospel in light of earliest Christian tradition. The doxological proclamation, *Alleluia*, expresses our receptivity to the gospel narrative of Jesus' mission.

The liturgy of the word reflects Luke's fundamental methodology—reflection on the present in light of Jesus' deeds and words as transmitted in tradition and articulated according to the scriptures. It does this in the life context of Christian worship.

Luke's narrative shows consummate handling of the story form and a delicate psychological sense of the dramatic, two qualities that invite the reader or listener to identify with the characters. Indeed, the gospel primarily communicates through this process of identification. Liturgically, this requires careful attention to the quality of oral interpretation. A good reading of the gospel should involve the assembly in the story and provide a point of departure for the homily. In Luke's perspective, God's Spirit thus continues to breathe life into the church.

Using this commentary

This book offers four kinds of commentary. The first is the extensive background analysis of the texts assigned for liturgical reading on Sundays and major feasts. The analysis is both literary and theological. It frequently situates a passage within the total work from which it comes. Passages are also related to the historical context for which they were written, presented in terms that should resonate in modern life. This dialogue between the conditions of life and the biblical response should provide homilists and others engaged in interpretation with a model for actualizing the text in the life of today's church.

For the responsorial psalm, the commentary highlights theological perspective and poetic movement in the verses selected and relates them to the community's response. The psalms generally prescind from a particular historical moment. They possess applicability over long periods of time, and their classic universality was respected.

Successive Sundays frequently draw texts from the same work, especially for the second and third readings. The commentary was written with a view to this continuity. In these cases it will be profitable to read the commentary on the preceding and subsequent passages along with the Sunday's unit.

The second type of commentary is the homily suggestions. Here a brief question or statement directly applies each reading to contemporary life. These suggestions focus on the hermeneutical question (what the scriptures mean today) as opposed to the exegetical question (what the scriptures meant at the time of writing). The suggestions aim to facilitate passing from past to present, and to obviate the danger of presenting exegesis in lieu of a genuine homily.

Third, each Sunday or feast has a short introduction that spells out some aspects of the relationship among the three readings. The introduction tries to synthesize the liturgy of the word. The relationship between the first and third readings is thematically clear and explicit. Since the second reading is assigned independently of them, its relation to the other two is based on the liturgical and life context. Usually it describes the ethical stance required of those who accept the gospel's challenge.

The fourth kind of commentary is more general: the introductions to the seasons of Advent, Christmas, Lent and Easter. They present the seasonal readings as a carefully orchestrated whole. Each Sunday contributes to an organic statement of the gospel from a season's perspective. These introductions will help the homilist by highlighting the season's point of departure, its progressive development and its climactic celebration. No Sunday can be isolated from the total liturgical effort to which it contributes.

These four types of commentary show that the liturgical interpretation of scripture cannot be reduced to other kinds of interpretation. The *Lectionary* mines its building blocks from the biblical quarry of the Old and New Testaments. But it constructively presents them within a new structure. Just as Luke drew on Mark's gospel and other sources to create a new gospel narrative, the church draws on Luke's gospel and related biblical texts to present a new gospel. In cycle C of the *Lectionary*, we have the liturgical gospel according to Luke.

Advent

Advent

The Advent Sundays provide a complete gospel, whose four units (Luke 21:25-28, 34-36; 3:1-6; 3:10-18; 1:39-45) are from Luke's historical theology of earliest Christianity. In their liturgical order (far different from their original context in Luke's work), these units present the gospel tradition from the point of view of Christian preparation for Christ's definitive coming.

Our Advent celebration begins with Luke's vision of the end and of Christ's coming in glory (Luke 21:25-28, 34-36). Our perspective is our present situation in Christian history. Just as the Old Testament looked forward to Christ's first coming, so now the church prays and lives for his final coming.

We continue our celebration by evoking the life and mission of John the Baptist who prepared Christ's first coming. In him the many centuries of prophetic history found a worthy climax. He is the model for Christians, to whom God's word now comes (Luke 3:1-6). We must present it as good news to the people, and recognize our humble position (Luke 3:10-18).

As Advent concludes, its meaning comes from Christ's consecrating presence, whose full deployment remains in the future (Luke 1:39-45). Christian history develops in progressive stages; but its significance and driving power spring from its consummation.

Like the Lukan gospel, our Advent gospel is formulated according to the scriptures. We see our celebration of promise and our active life of hope through the Old Testament expression of God's word. To this end, Jeremiah 33:14-16, Baruch 5:1-9, Zephaniah 3:14-18 and Micah 5:2-5 were selected as first readings.

Again, like the Lukan gospel, we affirm the earliest tradition that treated the basic issues of faith and life. In 1 Thessalonians 3:12-4:2, Philippians 1:4-6, 8-11, Philippians 4:4-7 and Hebrews 10:5-10, Paul and an unknown writer strengthen us in the way of life required for effective celebration of Christ's future coming.

First Sunday of Advent

Because life's ultimate goal is beyond history, the language of daily existence cannot express it. With Luke, we strain for verbal symbols and images that do not betray its heavenly reality (Luke 21:25-28, 34-36). That goal, however, is already revealed in history's promise. Jeremiah 33:14-16 penetrates history's surface and reveals its orientation to definitive life with God. Paul's prayer and ethical exhortation present the Christian way that brings history's hope to its definitive fulfillment (1 Thessalonians 3:12-4:2).

Jeremiah 33:14-16

The present passage is part of a later biblical editor's insertion (vv. 14-26) into the much older text of Jeremiah. It represents a post-exilic hope for an eternal Davidic dynasty to rule over Judah and for a perpetual priesthood to offer worship and sacrifice. These two institutions were seriously affected by the destruction of Jerusalem (587 B.C.) and the deportation to Babylon of all that was finest in Judah's population. These events notwithstanding, God who is just would continue to manifest his justice by fulfilling his promise to Israel and Judah.

The unit's fundamental concepts lie in the revelation of divine promise through Israel's history and in the reflection of God's justice in religious institutions. According to biblical tradition, both themes were articulated in terms of specific hopes, namely, the restoration of royalty and priesthood. Hope, however, was not extinguished when it failed to materialize in the expected manner. Justly founded, the fulfillment of God's promise continued to be sought in a spirit of openness. This attitude allowed for a later Christian interpretation of the passage in terms of the coming of Christ as Davidic royal messiah and unique high priest.

Psalm 25:4-5, 8-9, 10 and 14

In these verses from a personal lament, the psalmist prays for deliverance from his enemies. His prayer becomes ours as we ask God to give us his saving truth (vv. 4-5). We recognize we are sinners. Because God teaches his way to those who humbly admit their sinfulness (vv. 8-9), in kindness and constancy he will help us keep his covenant. We shall experience his friendship (vv. 10, 14). Together we proclaim, "To you, O Lord, I lift my soul."

1 Thessalonians 3:12--4:2

Paul's message to the young church of Thessalonica is cast against early Christian expectations of the imminent return of Christ. The passage includes: 1) the concluding prayerful wishes of a long thanksgiving passage (1:2—3:13) and 2) the introductory verses of the exhortation that follows (4:1—5:22).

The community needed strength and encouragement to grow in love for one another (3:12) and in holiness (3:13) in order to be well-prepared for Christ's coming. The source of this increase is the Lord Jesus himself; hence Paul's prayer. What Paul intended by holiness and love is developed in 4:3-8 and 4:9-12, respectively. The Old Testament law of holiness, "Be holy, for I, the Lord, your God, am holy" (Leviticus 19:2), is reinterpreted and applied in a Christian context. The same is true of the law of love (Deuteronomy 6:5; Leviticus 19:18), whose Christian expression is more familiar to us. Paul's understanding of the return of Christ is partly developed in 4:13—5:11.

Ultimately founded upon Christ's action, progress also depended on the community's own conduct which must be pleasing to God; hence, Paul's exhortation (4:1). In their efforts, the Thessalonians had the example of Paul's behavior in their midst (4:1) as well as the instructions he had given them (4:2).

The passage presents a theologically founded ethic for those living in expectation of the coming of the Lord.

Luke 21:25-28, 34-36

The gospel reading consists of two excerpts from an eschatological discourse attributed to Jesus (21:5-36). The entire passage is rich in the symbolic language and imagery of Jewish and Christian apocalyptic literature. Future ages are sharply telescoped and events of the present and recent past, like the destruction of Jerusalem, are viewed as signs of what is to come.

The signs of the end (vv. 25-26) lead to the coming of the Son of Man in power and glory (v. 27), a reference to the transcendent human figure of Daniel 7:13-14. As the signs begin to appear, there is no need for despair: they announce the faithful Christian's deliverance (v. 28). For his part, the Christian must live in a manner which prepares him to recognize the signs for what they are. Luke's reader must be attentive and pray for strength (vv. 34-36).

In earlier decades of Christian history, apocalyptic language frequently represented a real expectation of an imminent end of time. This cataclysmic event would involve the total transformation of creation and history into a new order. In this view, hope was to be placed not in earthly realities, which fail to reflect the goodness of their creator, but in God alone.

In the overall context of Luke's gospel, the end of history has been relegated to the distant future, and present life is seen to have positive value in a history of salvation. The language of apocalyptic has been retained with a force similar to that of hyperbole, heightening the reader's awareness of ultimate values in the present historical order and sensitizing him to an immediate response to God's transforming presence. The reader is asked to reflect not only on the end of history in general, but on the end of his own history, when present realities will indeed disintegrate for him and when finally he will stand before the Son of Man.

1. What are our advent expectations as compared with those of biblical times (Jeremiah 33:14-16)?

2. Like the early Christians, we must pay continuous attention to the signs of the times as we try to maintain an open-ended attitude toward the future (Luke 21:25-28, 34-36).

3. What are the essential elements of a Christian ethical attitude in light of the end of each one's world (1 Thessalonians 3:12-13)?

Second Sunday of Advent

In his life and message, John the Baptist embodied the advent hopes of Israel's long history of life with God. With Luke, we turn to John's prophetic mission to formulate our mission as we prepare for Christ's definitive coming (Luke 3:1-6). Baruch 5:1-9 stimulated Israel's hope for Jerusalem's restoration and now rekindles our hope for building God's lasting city. Paul's

*ebullient gratitude moves us to warm appreciation of the com-
munity relationships that support our efforts and bring them to
fruition (Philippians 1:4-6, 8-11).*

Baruch 5:1-9

We stand with the people of Israel at the threshold of Jerusalem's
restoration and look back to the days of Jerusalem's destruction and the
Babylonian exile. Actually, Jerusalem had long been restored, but the
author found it necessary to recall the hope that had accompanied the city's
resurrection at the heart of a new Israel.

Written in sharply articulated poetic verses, the passage means to
respond to current dulling of enthusiasm and to awaken in its readers that
same fervor which had inspired their forebears. To this end the author
recast and synthesized language well-known from the prophetic tradition
of Jeremiah and the book of Exodus. His main inspiration, however, came
from the book of Isaiah (cf. Isaiah 52:1; 61:10; 62:3; 1:26; 32:17; 49:22; 40:3-5;
41:19 in that order). The main theme of the new synthesis is that God's
splendor and glory are manifested in the life and worship of Jerusalem and
her people.

Psalm 126: 1-2, 2-3, 4-5, 6

The people finds itself deeply disturbed, threatened by misfortune. Our
meditation includes the whole of Psalm 126, which is divided into two
sections. In vv. 1-3, we join Israel in recalling the hopes and the joys once
ours. In vv. 4-6, we pray that our former good fortune be restored. Though
we plant in tears, we will reap in gladness. Our hope is based on past
experience, as expressed in the community response: "The Lord has done
great things for us; we are filled with joy."

Philippians 1:4-6, 8-11

After greeting the community, Paul wrote the warmest and the most
moving of the thanksgiving passages for which his letters are famous. The
reading does not include v. 7, which refers to Paul's historical situation as a
prison captive.

First, Paul speaks of the thanksgiving that accompanies his every
thought and prayer concerning the Philippians. His gratitude bears on
their unfailing work on behalf of the gospel from the time of their evange-

lization (vv. 3-5). Rejoicing in the community's gospel history, Paul affirms his confidence in the future: what God had begun in them would gradually be brought to completion by the day of Christ's full manifestation (v. 6).

Paul then turns to his love for the Philippians. In this he is giving new human expression to Christ's love. His affection for them has been sharpened by the pain of long separation and now manifests itself in genuine longing (v. 8). His feelings spill over into a prayer for them: growth in abundant love channeled into both understanding and experience. Thus enriched, their values will be properly focused (vv. 9-10).

The passage climaxes with a metaphorical summary: may the Christian harvest already ripening in the Philippians be truly rich in view of God's glory and praise (v. 11).

Luke 3:1-6

Luke identifies John as Zechariah's son, locates his activity in the desert and positions him in contemporary history. He amplified the simple manner of introducing the Old Testament prophets with a sweeping synchronism reminiscent of Greek historical writing. More precisely, it is not the prophet who is situated, but God's word spoken to him and through him from the moment he became a prophet (vv. 1-2).

The author summarizes John's work as a baptism accepted in repentance. Indirectly, John's baptism proclaimed the forgiveness of sins to which repentance was directed (v. 3).

Luke interprets John's work in light of the introduction to Deutero-Isaiah (vv. 4-6). The Isaiah passage (40:3-5) had also provided the basis for Baruch 5:7, today's first reading. John is compared to the royal road crews who prepared the Near East highways for a kingly visit. John's mission prepared the way for the manifestation of God's salvation in Christ.

> 1. As in Baruch's time, we must recall our origins to counter any dulling of our Christian enthusiasm (Baruch 5:1-9).
>
> 2. Genuine prayer directed to our neighbor's future must stem from actual Christian relationships (Philippians 1:8-10).
>
> 3. For Christians in a time of both fulfillment and advent, John the Baptist's life and work are a powerful message (Luke 3:1-6).

Third Sunday of Advent

Those who prepare the way can be mistaken for the one whose way they prepare. Luke's presentation of John keeps us from substituting the way for its goal (Luke 3:10-18). With Zephaniah we celebrate the ultimate renewal, already present to us in hope (3:14-18); with Paul we take on the selflessness that banishes anxiety, and we experience the peace of the Lord already near (Philippians 4:4-7).

Zephaniah 3:14-18

The prophet addresses the people of Judah during the reign of King Josiah (640-609), a time of major reform in the face of infidelity to the Mosaic law. Having reproached Jerusalem for her waywardness (3:1-10), he fixes his hope on a remnant of true Israelites (vv. 11-13). This hope leads to a song of joy calling Jerusalem to celebrate her coming renewal through the faithful few (3:14-18a).

The song looks to the future with firm hope. As the remnant emerges strong and faithful, Jerusalem will have nothing to fear. God himself will surely be in her midst. No longer under the negative judgment manifested by God's absence, Jerusalem will shout, sing and exult (vv. 14-15).

All reason for discouragement will have been dispelled with the Lord's coming as a mighty savior. He himself will rejoice with Jerusalem as he renews her in his love. The joy that awaits Jerusalem, which God will sing out over her, can be compared to the spirit frequently experienced in the celebration of Israel's festivals (vv. 16-18a).

Isaiah 12.2-3, 4, 5-6

The book of Isaiah's first part concludes with two short songs (12:1-3, 4-6). The first, a song of deliverance, affirms trust in God our salvation. The second is an invitation to thanksgiving, praise and joy. The first verse is not included in today's psalm. Verse 6 has inspired the communal response: "Cry out with joy and gladness: for among you is the great and Holy One of Israel."

Philippians 4:4-7

The passage is part of a series of exhortations (4:1-20) which climaxes in the doxology of 4:20. Rich in religious psychology, the relationships among the various attitudes must be carefully noted as well as their grounding in God's action in Christ Jesus.

True Christian rejoicing is an expression of selflessness. Paul exhorts the Philippi Christians to rejoice in the Lord, an attitude which must be made manifest before all. The basis is the Lord's nearness (vv. 4-5). His proximity also calls for the dismissal of anxiety.

Needs there are, and these must be recognized; but Christians should address them to God in prayer. Petition should recognize that God is already hearing their prayer. Their petitions should speak gratitude. Acknowledging their prayer is answered is not consonant with anxiety (v. 6).

With anxiety removed, God's peace will protect them in heart and mind. This peace comes from God, but its source transcends the life of the Christians. It is an experience that surpasses all understanding. Paul had greeted the Philippians with this peace in the liturgically inspired expressions of Philippians 1:2 and v. 7 of this reading. The passage is permeated with the hopeful expectation—*Marana Tha*, Come, Lord— that filled the early Christian liturgy.

Luke 3:10-18

As on the Second Sunday of Advent, the reading is from Luke's account of John the Baptist's ministry, the first part (3:1-22) of a unit on the preparation for Jesus' ministry (3:1—4:13).

The reading indicates John's message to various categories among those gathered to hear him, with a general statement concerning the relationship of John's mission to Jesus'. The passage had been prepared by more general expressions summarizing John's prophetic message (cf. especially vv. 7-9). These statements led directly to the questions asked by the crowds (vv. 10-11), the tax collectors (vv. 12-13) and the soldiers (v. 14). John speaks concretely, indicating what it meant for each to be a true offspring of Abraham. Taken as a whole, John's responses as well as his opening message explain the messianic expectations in his regard. Might John himself not be the messiah (v. 15)?

In vv. 16-17, John rectifies mistaken notions concerning his mission and directs attention to Jesus. Both John's person and his mission are far inferior to Jesus and his baptism in Spirit and fire. The reference to fire indicated the purifying work of the savior to come. It prepares the reader for the description of Jesus' role of judgment. John's mission prepares the people for a favorable judgment. Verse 18 is a concluding summary of John's message, an exhortatory proclamation of the good news.

1. Preparation for Christ's coming affects our responsibilities in life (Luke 3:10-14).

2. The advent attitude, hopeful expectation, characterizes Christian prayer (Philippians 4:4-7).

3. Awareness of God's presence, actual and imminent, dispels fear and renews in us the joy of God's love (Zephaniah 3:14-18).

Fourth Sunday of Advent

The Advent promise draws its meaning from the fulfillment of Christmas. Jesus' encounter with John relates Christ's coming, our goal, to our present yearning and efforts. As with John, our advent mission is consecrated by Christ's actual coming (Luke 1:39-45). Our striving is not a purely human effort but the work of God and his messiah (Micah 5:2-5). It is conducted within the new covenant, inaugurated by Christ but fulfilled in Christian living attuned to God's will (Hebrews 10:5-10).

Micah 5:2-5

The first reading is from the second part of the book of Micah (4:1—5:14). The prophet confronts Israel's fear before an expanding Assyrian empire during the 8th century B.C. (cf. vv. 4-5). The passage is divided into two parts; the first represents the prophet's view (vv. 2-4a), while the second sets out the view he opposes (vv. 4b-5).

In vv. 2-4a, the author focuses on Israel's true hope, God's action through his coming messiah. Verses 2-3 announce the birth of a strong shepherd who will preside over the return of those who have not been faithful to God and Israel's religious ideals. As the advent of peace (v. 4a), his greatness will extend to the ends of the earth.

The messianic prophecy heralds a new King David to be born in Bethlehem (cf. 5:1). It contrasts sharply with the remainder of v. 4 and v. 5, where hope is no longer placed in the Lord's messiah but in the people's military efforts. The latter verses should not be read in continuity with the preceding oracle. They show how Israel is *not* to respond to crisis. In v. 5, the expression "the land of Nimrod" is synonymous with "the land of Assyria" which now dominated Mesopotamia. It reflects Assyria's actual historical position; earlier Nimrod had symbolized Babylon's hegemony over the area (cf. Genesis 10:8-12).

Psalm 80:2-3, 15-16, 18-19

A stirring communal lament has provided the verses to express our urgent advent plea for Christ's coming. God is our shepherd; may he save us with power (vv. 2-3). God is the Lord of hosts; may he protect the vine of Israel he has planted (vv. 15-16). May he help the son of man (a title the New Testament applies to Jesus) and give us new life (vv. 18-19). These verses are punctuated by the community's hopeful prayer: "Lord, make us turn to you, let us see your face and we shall be saved."

Hebrews 10:5-10

In this extraordinary passage, the author focuses on the distinction between the old and the new covenant and on the superior quality of the new relationships which bind the people to God and to one another. The sacrifices of the old covenant had been prescribed by the law, but merely prefigured the one sacrifice of Jesus. Now that the former have been superseded, only the latter is pleasing to God.

Literarily, the author draws upon Psalm 40:7-9, but the Septuagint text varies somewhat from the Hebrew rendered in our versions of the psalter. He ascribes these verses to Jesus, who is made to interpret his life in sacrificial terms. Christ's self-offering consisted in the attunement of his will to God's.

Luke 1:39-45

The text presents the first of two meetings between Jesus and John the Baptist. This prenatal encounter forms part of Luke's effort to present John as the last in the line of Old Testament prophets. The second meeting would be at Jesus' baptism (cf. Luke 3:21-22).

As in the case of Jeremiah (1:5) and the servant in Isaiah 49:1, 5, God dedicated John for his prophetic role from his mother's womb. This statement of special providence on John's behalf was integrated into Luke's understanding of John's relationship to Christ. The main point is that John the forerunner was actually consecrated for his function by Christ. Both here and in the baptismal encounter, Christ comes to John and not John to Christ. This action is in keeping with the divine initiative which Christ mediates by his life and activity.

Since the precursor and the Christ are yet unborn, the author developed these themes by focusing on their mothers, who appear to be the main characters in the account. Elizabeth's response to Mary's greeting thematizes Jesus' superiority to her own son. It also draws our attention to the extraordinary dignity of the woman who accepted being "the servant of the Lord" (1:37) by becoming his mother (1:43).

1. What difference does Christ's coming really make in our life (Hebrews 10:5-10)?

2. As with John, Christ comes to us, not we to him; we have but to respond (Luke 1:39-45).

3. As we prepare for Christ's coming, our hope ultimately must be placed in God, not in our efforts (Micah 5:2-5).

Christmas

Christmas

The Christmas season begins with the feast and its three liturgical celebrations. Advent provided a gospel synthesis about Christ's future coming. The Christmas gospel focuses on Christ's presence, the fulfillment already attained in Christian history. Since that fulfillment is partial, it reaches out for the future and challenges us to participate in its unfolding. The Christmas season ends with the Lord's Baptism, when we join Jesus at the threshold of his mission (Luke 3:15-16, 21-22).

On Christmas, we celebrate the messiah's birth in relation to his divine origins and the manifestation of God's glory in his human life (Luke 2:1-14; 2:15-20; John 1:1-18). On the feast of the Holy Family, we celebrate Christ's coming in relation to his divine destiny and its attainment through the paschal mystery (Luke 2:41-52).

On the Solemnity of Mary, we reflect on Jesus' identity and function as revealed in his name, "the Lord is salvation" (Luke 2:16-21). Epiphany celebrates humanity's search for the messiah already in our midst. But we must acknowledge him in faith and find him in worship if we are to be saved (Matthew 2:1-12).

The Lord's Baptism occurs while Jesus is at prayer. Realized in the descent of the Spirit, it prefigures the coming of the Spirit on the church at Pentecost (Luke 3:15-16, 21-22).

The Christmas season leads us into the mystery of Christ's presence, celebrates its divine significance and salvific purpose, intimates the paschal and Pentecost mysteries and shows how we respond to that presence in our Christian mission. As in Advent, the church has provided us with a new gospel, the Christmas Gospel, whose units are arranged in a new and creative relationship, sparking reflection according to the scriptures in light of earliest tradition.

Christmas Mass at Midnight

In midnight darkness, we celebrate Jesus' birth with the first evangelists, simple shepherds (Luke 2:1-14). We yearn for Christ's coming in the future, but we rejoice that he is already with us in partial manifestation and promise. Isaiah 9:1-5 keeps our vision on the future, and Titus 2:11-14 presents the ethical demands of the Christmas celebration.

Isaiah 9:1-6

This messianic poem is one of the Immanuel prophecies (chapters 6-12). The author sings of a new king who will restore the glory of David's royal line. He looks with hope beyond the reign of weak Ahaz (763-716 B.C.) to a successor who will revitalize the Davidic ideals.

A metaphorical announcement opens the passage: light replaces darkness (9:1). The poet develops the metaphor in terms of human events: military threat to Jerusalem is over (9:2) for God has given the people joy (9:3-4). He indicates the source of hope: a king who will rule forever in justice and peace (9:6).

This new ruler will be prudent and wise ("Wonder-Counselor"), an instrument of God's protection ("God-Hero"). He will bring to the nation life ("Father-Forever") and peace ("Prince of Peace").

Psalm 96:1-2, 2-3, 11-12, 13

The psalm invites all to sing God's wonderful deeds day after day (vv. 1-3) as he comes to rule with justice and constancy (v. 13). All creation must rejoice and exult (vv. 11-12). The assembly responds with the reason, "Today is born our Savior, Christ the Lord."

Titus 2:11-14

The author may not have been Paul but he stood in the Pauline tradition. In 2:1-15, he gives Titus counsels on the attitude and behavior of types of Christians. The first concerns Titus, whose speech must be consistent with sound doctrine (2:1). This reading presents the doctrine, basis of Christian living.

God's grace in Christ extends to all (v. 11). However, as the offer of grace makes clear, its acceptance requires an ethical transformation (v. 12). Christ's self-giving was for our cleansing from everything that prevents us being his people (v. 14). This is the basis for living in the hope of Christ's full manifestation (v. 13). The passage demonstrates the way early Christians related practical morality and Christology.

Luke 2:1-14

In vv. 1-5, the author gives the historical context of Jesus' birth. In explaining the trip to Bethlehem, ancestral city of David's royal house, he emphasizes Jesus' messianic kingship. The early Christians interpreted the event in light of Micah 5:1, where Bethlehem's dignity as the birthplace of God's ruler in Israel is contrasted with its human insignificance (Matthew 2:6).

In vv. 6-7, this ironic contrast of divine wealth and human poverty is applied to Jesus' birth. As first-born, Jesus continues the royal name and inherits his ancestor's authority, responsibility and dignity. But Mary must place this new King David in a manger: even Bethlehem could not provide appropriate hospitality.

With the emphasis on Jesus' Davidic lineage, the pastoral scene of vv. 8-14 is appropriate. David had been Israel's shepherd king. Here, too, divine splendor meets humble humanity. Simple shepherds receive the message. The angelic manifestation directs attention to the good news: a savior, who is both Messiah (Christ) and Lord, has been born (vv. 10-11). Those who hear the gospel (v. 10) and turn to this savior (v. 12) are those on whom God's favor rests. They will enjoy God's own peace. This is God's glory (v. 14).

   1. Those who welcome the birth of Christ must live in the service of justice and peace (Isaiah 9:5-6; Luke 2:14).

   2. Those who celebrate the birth of Christ must live the way Christ did (Titus 2:11-14).

   3. The story of the incarnation (Luke 2:1-14), with its emphasis on divine wealth in the midst of human poverty, is also our story.

Christmas Mass at Dawn

At dawn, we respond to the good news, and become its first proclaimers (Luke 2:15-20). Like the shepherd-evangelists, we were empty and desolate; but we have become the city of God's

> *dwelling (Isaiah 62:11-12). We know our former state, and*
> *rejoice in God's merciful love (Titus 3:4-7).*

Isaiah 62:11-12

These verses conclude a poem from the time of Israel's deportation to Babylon. The author has already sung of the need for prayer (62:6-7), grounded in God's promise to reestablish Jerusalem (vv. 8-9). That prayer is about to be fulfilled (vv. 11-12), and he gives the order to rebuild the city.

The verses proclaim the coming of a savior for Zion. Jerusalem shall no longer be called "Forsaken" and "Desolate" (62:4) but "Frequented." This use of names reflects biblical antiquity's identification of the name with the reality. The liturgy applies the passage to Jesus. As savior, he transforms our city from a forsaken place into one throbbing with life.

Psalm 97:1, 6, 11-12

In this psalm of thanksgiving, we proclaim God's deeds by affirming his name. We rejoice in his destruction of evil (vv. 1, 6). In trust we sing the Lord's praise and accept the task of proclaiming his deeds before all (vv. 11-12).

Titus 3:4-7

Titus 3:1-8 is related to 2:1-15 (cf. Mass at Midnight). The author treats normative Christian behavior (3:1-2); but this time his attention focuses on relations with those outside the Christian community. As in 2:11-14, he indicates the theological basis of Christian morality (3:3-7).

He recalls the converts' former way of life (3:3), and develops the implications of God's salvation. God is our savior (v. 4) through Christ (v. 7). Our righteous deeds do not bring salvation. It is a gratuitous expression of God's kindness, love and mercy (v. 4). It was communicated to us through rebirth and renewal by the Holy Spirit in baptism (v. 5).

Luke 2:15-20

This passage must be read in light of Luke 2:1-14. The heavenly manifestation ends (v. 15a; cf. vv. 9, 13), and the author dwells on the shepherds' response to the angelic message. There are four phases. First, the shepherds resolved to go and see the event (v. 15b); second, they proceeded in haste and found the child in a manger (v. 16; cf. vv. 7, 12); third, having seen, they understood what they had been told (v. 17; cf. vv. 10-12, 14); fourth, having understood, they returned glorifying God (v. 20; cf. vv. 17, 9-14).

In the summary expressions of the fourth phase (v. 20), Luke deftly recapitulated the entire narrative, begun in 2:1. Between the third phase, when the shepherds came to faith (v. 17) and the fourth, in which they returned (v. 20), he anticipated their proclamation of the gospel events. Luke tells of everyone's astonishment at their report (v. 18). The narrative line focused on Mary had been suspended in v. 7. He now returns to it: Mary treasured and reflected on everything in her heart (v. 19).

> *1. If the human city is not to be "Desolate," Christians must be living signs of Christ's presence (Isaiah 62:11-12).*
>
> *2. Reborn in baptism, Christians share in the mystery of Christ's birth (Titus 3:5).*
>
> *3. The process that led the shepherds to proclaim the good news parallels the Christian's growth to mature faith (Luke 2:15-20).*

Christmas Mass During the Day

> *During the day, we celebrate the Word's ultimate revelation: the humanity of Jesus Christ (John 1:1-18). The "Word made flesh" is God's image, the climax of divine communication (Hebrews 1:1-6). We have good reason to proclaim God's rule, and we assume our responsibility to share his salvation (Isaiah 52:7 10).*

Isaiah 52:7-10

Several passages in Deutero-Isaiah (chapters 40-55; cf. especially 40:9-10) describe Israel's approaching liberation from Babylon in terms of the proclamation of good news of God's kingdom (52:7). The reference is to the Davidic kingdom through which God had ruled his people.

Shouts of joy greet the messenger for he heralds the restoration of Zion (v 8).) The poet-prophet calls out to the ruins of Jerusalem: break out in song! This invitation is based on the Lord's redemption of Jerusalem (v. 9). The Lord has manifested his power, so that all will see his salvation (v. 10).

Psalm 98:1, 2-3, 3-4, 5-6

The opening strophes of this hymn, similar to Psalm 96 (mass at midnight), sing of salvation and the revelation of justice. Our voices join with various instruments (vv. 5-6) to express the inexpressible.

Hebrews 1:1-6

In 1:1-4, the author divides history into two periods, the past and this final age. Divine revelation distinguishes the two. Formerly, God revealed himself in partial fashion through the prophets (v. 1). Now he has revealed himself fully in his Son (v. 2), perfect image of the Father (v. 3). With the emphasis on creation and glorification (vv. 2-3), this interpretation of Jesus is strikingly similar to John 1:1-18.

The introduction ends with a comparison between the Son's exalted status and the inferior status of angels (1:3). This contrast serves as a transition to the letter's first section.

John 1:1-18

The longer form of this reading is the prologue to John's gospel, composed from an early Christian hymn (probably vv. 1-5, 10-12a, 14 and 16) and supplementary prose narrative. Every verse in this prologue is rich in faith expression and understanding. This great synthesis of early Christian theology almost requires a study of the whole gospel!

The opening lines recall Genesis. The person of Jesus is part of God's inner meaning (vv. 1-2). The key term is "the Word," who moves out of God's life into creation, finite life and enduring light (vv. 3-5). In the centuries before the Word's incarnation, those who received the light were empowered to become God's children (vv. 10-12). Verse 14 proclaims that the Word has become flesh and dwelt among us. God's inner meaning and creative Word, manifested in history, became not a mere human word but the fleshly person of one who was God's only Son, filled with a love in which we all share (vv. 14b, 16).

The additions to the primitive hymn fall into three categories. First, they concern the relative role and message of John the Baptist (vv. 6-9, 15). Second, the author explains the expression "children of God," by applying the notion of virginal conception to all believers (vv. 12b, 13). Finally, the role of Jesus is contrasted with the law that prepared the full manifestation of God's love in Christ (vv. 17-18).

1. In order to proclaim the good news in truth, Christians must interiorize it first (Isaiah 52:7).

2. The Son is the perfect image of the Father (Hebrews 1:3). He has restored humanity, created in God's image but disfigured by sin.

3. God revealed himself not only in human actions and human words but in the very self and flesh of Christ (John 1:14).

Holy Family

The mystery of the Holy Family is inseparable from that of the greater Christian family. The gospel reading proves this with its emphasis on the preoccupations of early Christianity (Luke 2:41-52). In the second reading, we focus on the implications of Christian life for our family relationships (Colossians 3:12-21), following a long tradition of Israel's wisdom (Sirach 3:2-6, 12-14).

Sirach 3:3-7, 14-17

These two segments are from a collection of wisdom sayings on a young person's attitudes and duties toward parents. Verse 17a adds the first half of an unrelated saying introducing a collection on humility (vv. 17-28).

The sayings reflect the popular wisdom of the ancient Near East, but they include Israel's special sensitivity to life's religious dimensions. The author gives motives for respecting one's parents. Filial honor will be blessed (vv. 4-6); it has astonishing redemptive value (vv. 3, 14-15). Furthermore, it is the only attitude consistent with fear of the Lord (v. 7). A person who refuses to give this respect blasphemes God (v. 16).

Psalm 128:1-2, 3, 4-5

This short wisdom psalm extols (v. 1) those who recognize God as Lord and live accordingly. Their blessings are success in work (v. 2), a happy and fruitful household (vv. 3-4), and prosperity for Jerusalem (v. 5). The well-being of each person and each family is bound up with the community's well-being.

Colossians 3:12-21

After a general introduction on the Christian's relation to the risen Lord (3:1-4), and a section on behavior Christians must put aside (vv. 5-11), the author outlines the qualities of true Christian life (vv. 12-17). He applies this generic statement to the members of a Christian family (vv. 18-21).

The grounds for virtuous living consist in the Christians' state as God's chosen ones, holy and beloved (v. 12). Because they have been raised up in the company of Christ (3:1), the life of Christians must be an expression of Christ's word. If this word dwells in Christians (v. 16), all else will follow.

Paul exhorts wives to be submissive to their husbands and husbands to love their wives (vv. 18-19). In this he presumes the relation between husband and wife of his time. The emphasis on reciprocity (cf. also 1 Corinthians 7:3-5), however, reflects Paul's understanding that among Christians there is no distinction between male and female (Galatians 3:28). The unit concludes with directives for relations between parents and children (vv. 20-21).

Luke 2:41-52

In the context of Luke's gospel, the reading forms part of the concluding section (2:22-52) of the prologue (1:5-2:52). After presenting Jesus as the fulfillment of contemporary prophecy (2:22-40) and as clearly superior to prophetic life and activity in Israel (cf. 2:29), Luke shows him superior to the tradition of the sages active among Israel's teachers (2:46-47). Both parts of the narrative are situated in Jerusalem's temple but separated by the 12 years of Jesus' boyhood. At 13 Jesus would be considered an adult in the Jewish community.

Jesus' relationship to Israel's learned men is situated in the broader context of his relationship to his parents. Although born of a human family (cf. 2:1-21), Jesus is superior to his parents, relatives and acquaintances (v. 44). By his special relationship to his Father in whose house he chose to remain (v. 49), Jesus transcends his human parentage. With the narrative of Jesus' return to Nazareth with his parents (v. 51) and the summary concerning his subsequent growth (v. 52), Luke introduces us fully into the paradox of the incarnation.

As was customary for the Jews of that time, Jesus accompanied his parents to Jerusalem to celebrate the feast of Passover. The Passover, the loss of Jesus and the search for him, along with the finding on the third day (v. 46), evoke the mystery of Jesus' passion, death, burial and resurrection which took place at the time of Jesus' final Passover celebration. The Jesus of Luke's infancy narrative is the risen Lord, and the mystery of his incarnation, incomprehensible during Jesus' historical years (v. 50), can be understood only in light of Easter and the resurrection.

  1. *Family life is part of the covenant with God. Fidelity in love receives the blessings promised in the covenant (Sirach 3:3-7, 14-17).*

  2. *The word of God, incarnated in family living, must appear as love, respect, patience (Colossians 3:12-21).*

  3. *The resurrection enables us to grasp the mystery of the incarnation (Luke 2:46).*

Mary, Mother of God

Today's readings continue the celebration of Christmas by narrating the bestowal of Jesus' name (Luke 2:16-21), an event that fulfills the ancient blessing (Numbers 6:22-27). The second reading (Galatians 4:4-7) complements the gospel with the reason for the Lord's incarnation.

Numbers 6:22-27

Today's first reading, a priestly blessing of great beauty, is the last in a series of miscellaneous regulations (5:1-6:27), all introduced by "the Lord said to Moses." In each, the Lord's word is a command to address the Israelites (5:1, 5:11; 6:1) or Aaron and his sons (6:22).

The reading appears complicated, because it is a direct quotation within a direct quotation which is itself within a direct quotation! The innermost quotation is the blessing to be spoken by Aaron and his sons—by the priestly line that extends to the writers of the Torah (vv. 24-26). The blessing is quoted in Moses' statement on the manner of blessing (v. 23b). Finally, all of vv. 23b-26 is inserted in the Lord's word to Moses, including v. 23a, the order to speak, and v. 27, an indirect reiteration of the order and an assurance of blessing consequent on its fulfillment. The priestly blessing is endowed with both Mosaic and divine authority.

The blessing formula has three parallel statements, each with "the Lord" as subject of two verbs, and the Israelites as the blessing's beneficiaries. The expression "let his face shine upon you" (v. 25) is Hebrew idiom for "smile upon you," and indicates divine pleasure. The term "peace" (v. 26) implies all the benefits flowing from God's covenant with his people.

Psalm 67:2-3, 5, 6, 8

The meditative psalm opens with a blessing (v. 2) similar to the one in Numbers 6:22-27; but it applies this blessing beyond the Israelite community to all nations. God will be universally praised (vv. 3-4, 6), and all will rejoice in his mercy (v. 5). With Israel, today's assembly knows this prayer is already answered (v. 7), and responds with an antiphon inspired by vv. 2 and 8, "May God bless us in his mercy."

Galatians 4:4-7

Many centuries have passed since Christianity emerged from its Judaic origins. Most of us cannot imagine a time when the observance of Jewish practices was one of the basic issues confronting Christians. During the years of Paul's missionary activity, the question was widely debated. Even when a consensus was achieved in principle, practices continued to vary.

Paul himself was a strong advocate of freedom from the law. Soon after he evangelized the Galatians, however, Jewish Christians stirred up a reactionary movement in favor of Jewish observances. In this letter, Paul responds by reaffirming every Christian's freedom from the law.

In 4:1-7, the apostle contrasts two historical periods: our situation prior to Christ's coming, and the present time after he has delivered us from the law. Paul compares the former status to that of orphans who are not yet of age, a condition like that of a slave (vv. 1-3). Today's reading includes only the second part on the adult status of those who have received their inheritance in Christ (vv. 4-7).

Paul emphasizes the fully human condition of God's Son (v. 4). The reason he was born of a woman and under law was our deliverance from the law and slavery. He grants us the freedom of adopted sons (v. 5). The experiential proof is the spirit of God's Son in our hearts crying *Abba* ("Father"). In liturgical prayer we address God as Christ does (v. 6). Paul reaffirms his main point, the Galatian is no longer a slave but a son and an heir (v. 7).

Luke 2:16-21

The Christmas mass at dawn gave us Luke 2:15-20. Today's reading omits the statement introducing the shepherd's visit (v. 15) and adds the verse about Jesus' circumcision (v. 21).

Luke focuses on the bestowal of Jesus' name at the circumcision. The name Jesus, fairly widespread at the time, is the Greek form of Joshuah, meaning "Yahweh (the Lord) is salvation." Luke saw the name as symbolic of Jesus' role as savior (cf. 2:11). He indicates the name's providential significance by recalling its bestowal through a divine messenger (1:31).

1. God's blessing takes shape in human terms and images (Numbers 6:22-27).

2. Through the incarnation, God's Son enables us to become adopted sons and daughters of God (Galatians 4:4-7).

3. As his name indicates, Jesus is God's instrument of salvation (Luke 2:16-21).

Epiphany

Like the Jews, the gentiles also awaited Christ's coming. God had manifested himself in Israelite history in preparation for the messiah, but he had also revealed himself to the gentiles, bringing them to the unique messiah who would reign over all. Matthew 2:1-12 focuses on this confluence of divine revelation. Isaiah 60:1-5 represents only the Israelite response to that revelation. The gentile response, shrouded in mystery (Ephesians 3:2-3, 5-6), is now manifested in the visit of Abraham's non-Israelite descendants.

Isaiah 60:1-6

Isaiah 56-66 is a post-exilic addition to Deutero-Isaiah. These six verses are the first of three songs associated with the first return. All of them manifest the enthusiastic joy accompanying the promise of Israel's second exodus (chapters 40-55). This continuity appears in the strong literary allusions to Isaiah 40:18 and 22, easily seen in 60:4. In a special way, these songs proclaim the fulfillment of the good news of God's rule (40:9; 61:1).

Ecstatically appreciative of the new Jerusalem's glory, Isaiah 60:1-6 retains the universalist attitude nourished by the experience of the exile and developed in Deutero-Isaiah. The gentiles' response to Jerusalem's glory is lyrical, especially in vv. 3-6. Midian, Ephaph and Sheba (v. 6) represent Abraham's non-Israelite descendants (cf. Genesis 25:1-4) paying homage to "Zion of the Holy One of Israel" (v. 14). Sheba's gold and frankincense, the wealth of the nations, symbols of all that was finest, are offered to Jerusalem, "City of the Lord" (v. 14).

Psalm 72:1-2, 7-8, 10-11, 12-13

This royal psalm calls for blessings on the king. It views his reign as the manifestation on earth of God's heavenly rule, and reminds us of Christ the messianic king. Its evocation of foreign kings (vv. 10-11) makes it especially appropriate for today's feast. In the psalm's universality, the assembly responds, "Lord, every nation on earth will adore you."

Ephesians 3:2-3, 5-6

The liturgy reinterprets Isaiah 60:1-6 to proclaim Christ's universal manifestation. The Pauline letter to the Ephesians continues the theme. Although the letter was most probably not written by Paul himself, it certainly represents a highly developed synthesis of his thought.

Paul's ministry to the gentiles of Ephesus had been given him by God's goodness (v. 2) to manifest God's providential design (v. 3a), kept secret in ages past but now revealed (v. 5). The recipients of this revelation were the holy apostles and the prophets of the New Testament. These two ministries are frequently singled out in early Christian religious literature, both biblical and extra-biblical. Early in the second century, their functions, which Paul himself had shared, would be assumed by the presbyterate.

The mystery in question is the fact that the gentiles, by reason of their relationship with Christ Jesus, have now joined the Jews as members of Christ's body. They share in the promised inheritance. This relationship with Christ has come about through the preaching of the gospel (v. 6).

Matthew 2:1-12

Luke dwells lovingly on the scene of Jesus' birth at Bethlehem (2:6-7), but Matthew simply notes that Mary bore a son. Even this is quite secondary to the statements that Joseph had had no relations with her and that he named Mary's son Jesus (1:25). Luke subsequently focused on poor Jewish shepherds in the Bethlehem countryside (2:8-20). Matthew introduces magi, eastern astrologers, wealthy and learned men, gentiles with their roots in the ancient priestly caste of Persia (2:1-12). Luke's shepherds, previously oblivious to Jesus' birth, were led to Bethlehem by an angelic revelation. The magi observed Jesus' star, and were already in search of the king of the Jews. A discussion with Herod, one of their own social standing, leads them to Bethlehem.

These comparisons help us appreciate the uniqueness of Matthew's account. Beginning with the second chapter, he emphasizes Christ's manifestation to the gentiles. By presenting Christ as king, Matthew specifies the messianic role introduced at the conclusion of his genealogy (1:16-17).

The reading shows how an astrological theme, foreign to biblical thought, could be literarily integrated into a significant event, the response of the gentiles to Christ. Even gentile religions prepared the way for Christ.

1. Contact with men and women outside the church awakens in us a sense of universal mission (Isaiah 60:1-6).

2. God's work in history unfolds gradually; it is for us to manifest its meaning (Ephesians 3:2-3, 5-6).

3. Non-Christians are led to Christ from within their own culture. We must respect that experience and present Christ in relation to it (Matthew 2:1-12).

Baptism of the Lord

God's creative Spirit, manifested in Jesus' work, energizes the church and all who participate in her work of salvation. With Luke we reflect on how this Spirit distinguishes the Christian mission from all that prepared it (Luke 3:15-16, 21-22). Isaiah 42:1-4, 6-7 spells out the prophetic hope that looked to the Spirit's manifestation in God's servant. In Acts 10:34-38 we see the Spirit in relation to Jesus' work and to the church's challenge to reach out to all peoples in the gospel mission.

Isaiah 42:1-4, 6-7

In this reading, the liturgy presents the first of the Isaiah poems known as the songs of the suffering servant (42:1-4). Skipping the introductory v. 5, it adds the first two verses (vv. 6-7) of the prophet-poet's lyrical application of the basic theme of justice (vv. 6-9). Verses 5-7 are so closely related to the song that they can constitute its conclusion.

Like Moses, David and other great figures in Israelite history, the servant is God's chosen one (v. 1), typifying what was finest in Israel's life and spirit. The words spoken by the divine voice at Jesus' baptism adapt 42:1a to him (cf. gospel). God has invested the servant with his spirit. This creative and life-giving power enables the servant to establish a reign of justice, not only in Israel but even among the gentile nations (42:1b, 4). God's chosen will accomplish this quietly, gently, without violence (vv. 2-3).

The meditative prolongation in vv. 6-7 is closely related to Isaiah 61:1; but like the song in 42:1-4 the text emphasizes the servant's universal mission. It also introduces the notion of covenant (v. 6), one of the most significant social images in ancient Israelite theology. Its meaning is well expressed in the repeatedly quoted expression: "I will be your God, and you shall be my people."

Psalm 29:1-2, 3-4, 3, 9-10

Because the experience of God is manifold, the psalms reach for graphic images to express it. In psalm 29, God is presented in images associated with the ancient Near East's storm lord. A call to give glory to God (vv. 1-2) is followed by a description of his voice over the waters (vv. 3-4). His glorious manifestation calls forth our acclamation (vv. 3, 9-10). By contrast, the community response affirms, "The Lord will bless his people with peace."

Acts 10:34-38

The events surrounding the evangelization and baptism of Cornelius' household constitute a major turning point in Acts' account of the early church. The gospel message first proclaimed to the Jews is now addressed to the gentiles. This reading is from the opening section of the discourse attributed to Peter on this decisive occasion.

In the introduction, Peter reflects on the Christian mission's universal scope. His encounter with Cornelius and his relatives and friends (10:24) shows him that all who fear God and act rightly are acceptable (vv. 34-35). Peter is then made to summarize Luke's gospel, beginning with a statement of God's message proclaimed through Jesus Christ. That message was the good news of peace. Although the gospel was first announced to Israel, it was destined even for the gentiles, since Jesus is Lord of all (v. 36). Peter turns to Jesus' life. His prefatory expression, "I take it you know," is addressed primarily to the readers rather than to Cornelius, since the latter was clearly ignorant of Jesus' life, albeit open to learn (vv. 30-33). Selection of this passage for today's liturgy was determined by vv. 37-38, a reference to the baptism John preached and to Jesus' anointing by the Holy Spirit.

In order to show the divine origins of Jesus' mission, Luke omits any hint that Jesus was actually baptized by John. He focuses on how God anointed Jesus with the Holy Spirit and with power (v. 38).

Luke 3:15-16, 21-22

Two short segments from Luke's presentation of John the Baptist are background for Jesus' public ministry. In the first, John responds to the people's messianic expectations by comparing his baptism to the superior baptism effected by Jesus (cf. gospel, p. 16). The second refers to Jesus' baptism and the accompanyuing events (vv. 21-22).

Brief as they are, the last two verses are extremely rich in Luke's understanding of Jesus' meaning. Jesus' baptism is barely mentioned, in a subordinate clause indicating the baptism had already taken place. Luke carefully distinguishes Jesus from all others who had been baptized, and shows him now at prayer. This clause introduces the theophany, the passage's central concern. The description of this draws upon two passages from Isaiah.

The first is in a prayer for God's favor, more specifically for a great redemptive act similar to Israel's exodus from Egypt. In Isaiah 63:19, the poet prays God to "rend the heavens and come down." In place of "rend," the Septuagint has "open" and this is the reading in Luke 3:21. The descent of God's Spirit upon Jesus is the answer to Isaiah's prayer and also a promise, because the Spirit would later descend on the community of Jesus' followers at Pentecost.

The second text is Isaiah 42:1, the opening verse of the first of the songs of the suffering servant (42:1-4), today's first reading. In place of "servant," however, the Lukan voice from heaven declares Jesus to be God's Son. Like the servant in Isaiah, Jesus would indeed suffer. But, he is more than God's servant. "Son" is a clear reference to Jesus' divine status.

> *1. Israel's promise of a covenant of peace is the biblical setting for Jesus' mission (Isaiah 42:1-4, 6-7).*
>
> *2. The true source of Jesus' life-work was his anointing by the Holy Spirit (Acts 10:38).*
>
> *3. The fulfillment of the Old Testament comes in response to Jesus' prayer after his baptism (Luke 3:21-22).*

Lent

Lent

The Lenten gospel forms Christians in the midst of the human condition. Sin, death and God's absence cannot be denied, but neither can repentance, life and the divine presence. In Christ's person, God extends hope to all who join the commitment to pass through death to resurrection's glory. In his teaching and his gentle but firm dealing with struggling sinners, Christ shows us how to continue his saving mission in history.

Lent invites us to confront ultimate human realities, to accept Christ's call to change mind and heart and take up the Christian challenge. It provides a formative program for catechumens as well as a renewal experience for the baptized, now called to accept new members into the Christian community.

The first two Sundays juxtapose the two major poles of Christian life—confrontation with evil (Luke 4:1-13) in view of enjoying God's full glory (Luke 9:28-36). This mystery of death to sin and life in God is also presented at Lent's end in the passion celebration (Luke 22:14-23:56) and in Lent's climax on Easter (John 20:1-9). The Easter feast is the conclusion of Lent and the beginning of the Easter season. As we learn on Lent's second Sunday, Christ's passion and our struggle with evil must always be viewed in the light of his rising to glory.

On the Third, Fourth and Fifth Sundays of Lent, we join the first disciples in three concrete episodes; we observe Jesus' behavior and hear his teaching. Repentance is necessary and possible for all (Luke 13:1-9). Though we are sinners, we are welcome at Christ's table. We must rejoice as other sinners join us there (Luke 15:1-3, 11-32). Since all are sinners, no one has the right to discriminate against others or seek their death. With Christ we humbly sound the call to conversion and sinlessness (John 8:1-11).

As in the Advent and Christmas seasons, the first and second readings of Lent have been carefully selected to provide a full and balanced teaching. Our Lenten renewal echoes ancient Israel's faith experience and takes up the challenge of early Christian tradition.

First Sunday of Lent

> *Ultimately, Jesus' life is a resounding victory over the forces of evil. In Luke 4:1-13, we stand with him as he experiences Israel's classic temptations and rejects what distorts his identity and betrays his mission. Jesus' stance is grounded in God's salvific work on Israel's behalf, proclaimed in Old Testament faith (Deuteronomy 26:4-10) and manifested in Jesus' resurrection, extended to all who confess Christ as Lord (Romans 10:8-13).*

Deuteronomy 26:4-10

The brief Israelite creed (Deuteronomy 26:5-9) is the best known portion of Moses' testament, the major part of the book of Deuteronomy. The creed is the expression of faith spoken by one who brings the harvest's firstfruits to the temple in recognition of God's gift of land and crops (vv. 4,10).

In the creed, the devout Israelite identifies with his patriarchal ancestors, Abraham, Isaac and Jacob ("my father"). Historical solidarity, a fundamental biblical attitude, extends to every phase of Israelite history, from the days in Egypt to the blessings and security of the promised land. The continuum reaches to the present moment to include the history of the person who professes faith through the ancient creed.

The creed begins with the first person singular, "my" (v. 5), but continues with the first person plural, "us," "we," "our" (vv. 6-9). The Israelite was acutely aware of his relationship to the community from which he drew his identity. The personal profession of faith was spoken out of the community by one who saw himself as a member of God's people.

The liturgy uses the passage as a good example of a proper response to trial and difficulty (vv. 6-7). God is ever present to deliver his people (vv. 7b-9), a complex theme developed in today's gospel.

Psalm 91:1-2, 10-11, 12-13, 14-15

This wisdom psalm provides a meditation on the divine protector. An invitation to trusting prayer (vv. 1-2) is followed by a promise of protection (vv. 10-11) and a symbolic description of what God will do for the faithful (vv. 12-13). The psalm concludes with an oracular pronouncement in which God assures us he will answer our prayer and deliver us (vv. 14-15). The community's stance is prayerful: "Be with me, Lord, when I am in trouble."

Romans 10:8-13

Today's first reading is part of Paul's biblical theology of God's universal offer of salvation (Romans 9-11). For faith to be salvific, it must not only live in the believer's heart but be actively professed in the confession of Christ as Lord.

Belief that God raised Christ from the dead (vv. 8-9) may be a source of justification, but only its public verbal expression leads to salvation (v. 10). There is no distinction in the object of faith, which remains the gospel preached by Paul. Justifying and salvific faith are two intimately related stages in a person's acceptance of faith.

In Paul's understanding, faith is inseparable from the individual's community relationships, and salvation is linked with the communication of faith to others. For Paul the call to be a Christian is at one and the same time a call to Christian mission.

After this explanation, Paul argues from Isaiah 28:16 (v. 11) and Joel 3:5 (v. 13), developing his teaching to include both Jew and Greek (v. 12).

Luke 4:1-13

On this first Sunday of Lent, the gospel challenges the Christian community to reflect on its mission and to reject unequivocally the fundamental temptations that would destroy it. Jesus provides a powerful model of the right attitude.

Even as Son of God (Luke 3:22, 38) and Spirit-filled (3:22; 4-1), Jesus was actually tempted. Indeed, the Spirit led Jesus into the place of temptation (4:1). The narrative reveals Jesus at grips with the power of evil, objectified in the person of the devil. Like Mark (1:12-13), Luke indicates the significance of Jesus' 40-day temptation by relating it to Israel's great time of testing in the desert experience (Deuteronomy 8:2).

Three times the devil tempts Jesus, and three times Jesus responds with the classical language of scripture. Each temptation bears directly on the nature of Jesus' mission. What does it mean for Jesus to be Son of God (4:3, 9)? What is the true nature of the messianic kingdom (4:5-6)?

The first temptation confronts Jesus with the easy way of the miracle-worker. Jesus responds with Deuteronomy 8:3, clarifying the human dimensions of his mission. At the same time, his answer broadens the scope of human needs to include other than earthbound realities (vv. 3-4).

In the second temptation, the devil focuses on political dominion. Because Jesus' kingdom is not of this world, political power would have required the worship of evil. Jesus rejects political messianism with Deuteronomy 6:13—worship is for God alone (vv. 5-8).

The third temptation involves the true meaning of Jerusalem and its temple worship. In keeping with the temptation's religious nature, the devil now quotes scripture (Psalm 91:11-12). With Deuteronomy 6:16, Jesus rejects a basic distortion in humanity's relationship with God. Testing God is a rejection of the ordinary human condition as well as an effort to force God to supply what must be our responsibility (vv. 9-12).

With this, the tempting is complete. The vanquished devil departs (v. 13) and Jesus is ready to move to Galilee for the beginning of his mission (4:14 ff). The devil, however, awaits another opportunity (v. 13).

1. Two essential characteristics of biblical faith, historical solidarity and community consciousness, challenge us today (Deuteronomy 26:5-9).

2. Since we are saved by saving others, living faith must be publicly professed (Romans 10:8-13).

3. Jesus' response to temptation is a norm for us as we respond to our fundamental temptations (Luke 4:1-13).

Second Sunday of Lent

Glory awaits those who join Christ in his victory over evil. This vision must not be an escape but a stimulant for our mission in history. With Luke we accept Jesus' exodus from history and take up the Christian way (Luke 9:28-36). Jesus' transfiguration and its focus on his exodus (ascension) was prepared by God's promise to Abraham and the covenant God offered him (Genesis 15:5-12, 17-18). In Jesus' departure from history and ascension to God, those promises are fulfilled (Luke

*24:50-53) and extended to all nations. We join Paul in assuring
the universality of the gospel blessing (Philippians 3:17-4:1).*

Genesis 15:5-12, 17-18

The unit develops two major biblical themes, God's promises to Abraham (vv. 5-8) and the Abrahamic covenant (vv. 9-12, 17-18). The omitted verses (13-16) are a later insertion to account for the long delay in the fulfillment of the promises.

In a brief dialogue, God presents the two promises: Abraham will have numerous descendants (v. 5) and they shall possess a land of their own (v. 7). To appreciate these promises, we should recall that Abraham and Sarah were already very old, and as Hebrews they had no right to own land. Abraham met the first promise with faith (v. 6); for the second he requested a sign (v. 8).

In answer, God offered Abraham a covenant (vv. 9-12, 17-18). Stark, primitive and heroic in its symbols, the covenant ritual evokes the awesome simplicity of ancient patriarchal religions: animals slaughtered and halved, birds of prey swooping down on the carcasses, sunset, trance, darkness, smoking brazier, flaming torch. Abraham's struggle with the birds of prey is symbolic of what threatens the covenant. God's flaming passage through the sacrificed animals symbolizes his willingness to be killed should he not abide by his covenant promise. God could not have affirmed his promise more emphatically.

This covenant was the second in a series (Noah, Abraham, Moses). For all its primitiveness, it expresses the foundation stones of biblical faith, namely, that our relationship to God is personal and historical. Each stage of covenant history is a step toward restoring the harmony first established at creation.

Psalm 27:1, 7-8, 8-9, 13-14

The psalm is composed of a song of trust (vv. 1-6) and a personal lament (vv. 7-14). Our meditation begins with the introductory verse of the former. Since God is my light, salvation and refuge, whom could I possibly fear? We continue with verses from the lament. God seems to be absent. We cry to have his response (vv. 7-8), and to know his presence once again (vv. 8-9). We confidently believe our prayer will be answered (vv. 13-14). In response we take up the opening verse: "The Lord is my light and my salvation."

Philippians 3:17-4:1

The passage is part of a longer unit (3:2-4:3) in which Paul warns the Philippians against those who would transform Christianity into a form of Judaism. At issue was the universal, non-ethnic nature of the early churches.

To be a Christian, one need not be Jewish (3:2-3). In support of this widely accepted but contested position, Paul recalls his Jewish origins and former religious spirit. Great as these were, he now counts them as nothing in the light of Christ (3:4-16; cf. p. 53 for vv. 8-14). With this in mind Paul urges his readers to be imitators of him (3:17).

Imitation of the apostle is an important element in Paul's pastoral theology (cf. 4:9; 1 Thessalonians 1:6; 2 Thessalonians 3:7, 9; etc.). Such imitation can be called for insofar as Paul himself was an imitator of Christ Jesus (1 Corinthians 11:1). The exhortation does not imply the Christian must try to be other than himself or herself. On the contrary, by becoming fully ourselves in Christ we are like Paul. The two coincide. Paul's example helps us on the way.

In vv. 18-19, Paul describes attitudes and behavior contrasting with his own. These lead to death, but the Christian must set his hope on life and future glorification with Christ (vv. 20-21).

Luke 9:28-36

Like Mark and Matthew, Luke relates the transfiguration of Jesus to Peter's profession of messianic faith (9:18-21), a prediction of the coming passion-death-resurrection (9:22), the Christian call to suffering discipleship (9:23-26) and Jesus' promise that some with him would not taste death before seeing God's reign (9:27).

Whatever the interpretation of that promise in earlier tradition, its fulfillment is now seen in the transfiguration, a manifestation of God's reign. Called to proclaim their faith and to follow in the way of Jesus' cross, his followers shall also share in his glory.

The reading describes a Christophany, a manifestation of Christ's divine glory analogous to the great theophanies accompanying the covenant with Abraham (Genesis 15) and Israel's invitation to covenant at Sinai (Exodus 19:16-25). Other examples are the prophetic calls of Isaiah (6:1-13) and Ezekiel (1:4-28). Earlier in the New Testament, we have Jesus' baptism (Luke 3:21-22).

In the synoptic accounts of Jesus' transfiguration, Moses and Elijah appear as symbols of the law and the prophets now fulfilled in Jesus. There is another aspect to their significance. According to tradition, both figures had been assumed into heaven, to return at the consummation of time. For Mark and Matthew, they are a symbolic promise of Jesus' return or second coming. Luke focuses on their going away or assumption.

Only Luke gives us the subject of conversation, namely, Jesus' exodus (9:31). Their presence symbolizes Jesus' ascension. In Luke's view, it was essential that Christians accept the ascension and the concomitant absence of the historical Jesus in order to discover his transformed presence in the Christian community.

1. In both the Old and New Testaments, a covenant is a personal relationship between God and people. The relationship must be expressed in culturally adequate symbols, but no symbol can supply for a non-existent relationship (Genesis 15:9-12, 18-17).

2. Like Paul, our lives must express something of Christ Jesus' life, to provide a live transmission of tradition, the church's life (Philippians 3:17-4:1).

3. With Luke's readers, we must come to terms with the departure (exodus) and consequent absence of the historical Jesus if we are to assume our responsibility as his followers (Luke 9:28-36).

Third Sunday of Lent

Tragic events in life and history may not be divine punishments for sin, but they stand as models of what will happen to the sinner who rejects the final chance to repent. Luke's message in 13:1-9 is for all who meet God in life's purifying fire and discover he is ever with them (Exodus 3:1-8, 13-15). God's gift is not automatically salvific. It must become incarnate in the human response in order to bring us to life (1 Corinthians 10:1-6, 10-12).

Exodus 3:1-8, 13-15

The reading, from the narrative of Moses' vocation and mission, includes features characteristic of the prophetic call of people like Isaiah (see p. 96) and Ezekiel. It also resembles God's offer of a covenant relationship to Israel.

A brief introduction situates the episode at Horeb, a traditional name for Sinai, where the angel of the Lord appears to Moses in a flaming bush. As the rest of the narrative indicates, the "angel" must be understood as God's self-manifestation, and not as a personal being distinct from God. The flame evokes God's purifying holiness. Since the place is holy (vv. 1, 5), the bush remains unconsumed.

God calls Moses by name, and Moses indicates a ready attitude: "Here I am!" This affirmation of Moses' presence to God prepares us for the development of God's presence to Moses and his people. The latter presence is affirmed in terms of the fathers and subsequent history, and the revelation of the divine name.

In vv. 5-8, God introduces himself as one present to Abraham, Isaac and Jacob, known in their experience. The same God has now observed his people's affliction in Egypt and he will deliver them. God's ancient promise to Abraham of a land in which his people would prosper is about to be fulfilled (see p. 45). Verses 9-12 (omitted) narrate Moses' mission in bringing God's people out of Egypt.

In vv. 13-14, God gives his name, "I am who am," from which we obtain "Yahweh." In v. 15 Yahweh is equated with the God of the fathers. The text does not present the incident as the first revelation of Yahweh's name. But it is the name by which Israel will now know God. Whatever may be its original meaning (perhaps "I am the one who causes you to be") the present context requires "I am the one who is with you" (v. 12).

Psalm 103:1-2, 3-4, 6-7, 8 and 11

A psalm of thanksgiving for God's healing pardon speaks our joyful blessing (vv. 1-2). What God has done reflects his unchanging will to redeem our lives from destruction (vv. 3-4). As he showed Moses and the Israelites, he allows no injustice to go unrighted (vv. 6-7), because his merciful love transcends the human level (vv. 8, 11). The communal response summarizes the divine attitude: "The Lord is kind and merciful."

1 Corinthians 10:1-6, 10-12

This extremely powerful argument is based on Old Testament history. Its point is Christians cannot remain content with the fact that they have been graced and now stand upright. They must watch lest they fall (v. 12), especially in the conflict that accompanies the end of the ages (v. 11).

Paul compares the Christians to the ancient Israelites, "our fathers" (v. 1). In a way, the Israelites had been baptized, and they too had enjoyed a spiritual food and drink (vv. 2-4). To no avail (v. 5)! Christians should not expect automatic results of Christian baptism and eucharist. In this respect, Paul saw two dangers at Corinth. First, the quality of the eucharistic assembly frequently plummeted to the point of a counter-sacrament. Second, in their complacency, the Christians failed to see their eucharist was frequently of no value (cf. 1 Corinthians 11:17-34).

For these sacramental actions to be effective, they must reflect the participants' attitudes, in accord with the sacrament's meaning. Referring to Numbers 14:16, where the Israelites are struck down by God for their revolt in the desert, Paul indicates this occurred as an example for us (vv. 6, 11). If we behave like the Israelites, even with baptism and eucharist, we shall suffer their lot. Verses 7-9, here omitted, include three examples of reprehensible behavior we must not imitate.

Luke 13:1-9

Today's third reading includes a brief Lukan presentation of Jesus' call to reform (vv. 1-5) and a parable about a barren fig tree (vv. 6-9). The former contains two incidents otherwise unattested in the New Testament. The latter is a Lukan substitution for the Markan episode in which Jesus curses a barren fig tree (Mark 11:12-14, 20-25; cf. Matthew 21:18-22).

Two tragic incidents from recent history are adduced by Jesus to provoke reflection on sin and punishment. Contrary to certain ancient beliefs and doubtless in response to popular opinion, Jesus asserts there is no equation between sin and earthly suffering. The Galilean and Siloam incidents are no commentary on the life of those who died. However, unless Jesus' hearers reform their lives, they will meet the same end. The implication is that, just as all are sinners, all are called to reform. Failure to repent will bring death regardless of the relative gravity of one's past sin. Life or death depends on our response to Christ, not on the greatness of our sin.

The severity of the Markan episode concerning the curse of the fig tree is tempered by Luke. He refused to include this harsh judgment on the Jewish nation and substituted a parable. This parable, which may allude to the three-year duration of Jesus' mission (v. 7), does not end in condemnation but in the vinedresser's request that the owner grant him another year's effort. There is a chance that the plant may yet be fruitful.

The unit is an appeal to repentance, warning the reader of failure to heed Jesus' call. At the same time it shows God's judgment tempered by mercy.

> 1. *Unless we see God as personally present with us (Exodus 3:13-15), as the God of our heroic ancestors in the faith (Exodus 3:1-8), Exodus 3:1-15 will remain meaningless.*
>
> 2. *Is our eucharist a counter sign, expressing the opposite of what the eucharist must be (1 Corinthians 10:1-6, 10-12)?*
>
> 3. *Does our tendency to "write off" various people in the church correspond to the parable of the barren fig tree (Luke 13:6-9)?*

Fourth Sunday of Lent

> *We must not murmur but rejoice at the sinner's recovery and return to life. With Jesus' parable in Luke 15:11-32, we renounce our tendency to criticize his association with sinners (Luke 15:1-3). Ours is a ministry of reconciliation (2 Corinthians 5:17-21) that calls for regular renewal of the covenant relationship, grounded in Israel's great covenant experiences in the Old Testament (Joshua 5:9, 10-12).*

Joshua 5:9, 10-12

Verse 9 is the literary conclusion of a unit on the circumcision of the Israelites after their crossing into the promised land. The long 40-year wandering in the desert was over.

Verses 10-12 present the first Passover celebration in their new land. In its present form, the text presupposes that the primitive feasts of Passover and Unleavened Bread have merged. Earlier, however, and at the exodus, the two were distinct, representing spring festivals for vastly different cultural contexts. Passover was the feast of pastoral peoples, hence the sacrifice of lambs. The feast of Unleavened Bread was agrarian, a harvest festival. (In Israel harvest coincides with the end of spring.) As Israel gradually transformed from a nomadic to a sedentary people, the two feasts, celebrated at the same time of year, naturally became one festival.

With time, they assumed new significance. Rather than a celebration of spring's annual cycle, they became closely associated with Israel's liberation from Egypt and the passage through the desert into the promised land. The historicized feast became closely attuned to the basic thrust of Israelite religion, whose God was not only creation's Lord, but an historically involved God. With this historical and theological meaning in mind the author describes the celebration.

Psalm 34:2-3, 4-5, 6-7

A thanksgiving psalm provides verses for our meditation. We bless the Lord and expect the lowly to join us (vv. 2-3), because he has delivered us from slavery (vv. 4-5). Ours is a saving God, and we must turn to him joyfully and unblushingly (vv. 6-7). The community invites everyone, "Taste and see the goodness of the Lord."

2 Corinthians 5:17-21

The second reading presents Paul's work as a ministry of reconciliation. The conflict at Corinth invited this view of Paul's ministry. As often happens, a concrete event frequently sensitizes Paul and others to a universal value in Christianity.

It was no longer possible to view the Corinthians according to a merely human standard. In Christ, they had become a new creation. With this expression, Paul attempted to convey the extraordinary value and transforming power of the Christian's relationship (v. 17) to Christ.

The new creation had been effected by a divine act of reconciliation. Jesus' entire mission had been one of reconciliation. In this, however, he was God's agent; it is God who reconciled us through Christ and extended to us a share in Christ's ministerial role (v. 18).

In v. 19 Paul clarifies his prior statement. God's work of reconciliation was already accomplished through Christ. What Paul has been entrusted with is the *message* of reconciliation, that is, the good news that God has effected reconciliation through Christ. Paul does not stand alongside Christ in the ministry but serves as his ambassador. Through Paul, God appeals for an affirmative response to a gesture already made (v. 20a). In the latter half of vv. 20 and 21, Paul gives direct expression to the ministry he attempted to clarify.

Luke 15:1-3, 11-32

When sinners gathered around Jesus (v. 1), those recognized as righteous (or who thought themselves so) expressed their dismay at Jesus' eating with sinners (v. 2). Sharing a meal was an important gesture expressing peace, solidarity and fellowship among the participants. How then could Jesus welcome sinners to table fellowship? He responded with three parables. The third and longest, the story of the prodigal son, is in today's reading (vv. 11-32).

We must not reduce this parable to an abstract statement on God's merciful dealings with sinners. Had this been Jesus' or Luke's intention, a moral principle would have sufficed. Instead, we have a story with several characters whose relationships develop through the plot's unfolding. The parable communicates through our identification with each character. All can recognize the way of the prodigal, the welcome of the father, and the pique of the elder son in their own experience. The parable is a mirror of our concrete ethical complexity and requires that we position ourselves with regard to each of its typical characters and their roles.

As we enter the story's movement, our attitude is transformed—unless we resist the gospel—to understand why Jesus ate with sinners and why we must allow him to reach out once again to sinners through our table fellowship.

> *1. We must pause at life's major turnings and celebrate God's abiding presence to us (Joshua 5:10-12).*
>
> *2. Every Christian is engaged in God's work of reconciliation through Christ (2 Corinthians 5:17-21).*
>
> *3. How is our attitude toward "sinners" at eucharistic table fellowship challenged by Jesus (Luke 15:1-3, 11-32)?*

Fifth Sunday of Lent

> *The sinner must not be destroyed but welcomed to new life in Christ. Jesus' response to the adulteress consoles us and shows us how we must treat others (John 8:1-11). No one is imprisoned by the past. Like the divine promise of salvation, Christians look to the future (Isaiah 43:16-21), when God will reduce past failures and limitations to insignificance (Philippians 3:8-14).*

Isaiah 43:16-21

The passage is from a series of poetic promises in which God announces a new redemption and restoration of Israel. God is identified in terms of his past extraordinary deeds on Israel's behalf (vv. 16-17). We recognize the events of exodus at the crossing of the Reed Sea. However, Israel must not focus on past events (v. 18) because God is about to do something new (v. 19a).

This word was addressed to Israel in exile at Babylon. Deutero-Isaiah compares this situation to Israel's servitude prior to the exodus. Correspondingly, the return from Babylon will be like a new exodus. We also find a rich mixture of creation themes. The new exodus will be like a new creation (vv. 19b-21).

Through clever use of concrete, highly visual language, the passage evokes the imminence of the deliverance. The reading ends by noting the purpose of God's action on Israel's behalf, that they might announce his praise. For a greater appreciation of the present unit, read Isaiah 40:1-11, the introduction to Isaiah 40-55 (Deutero-Isaiah).

In passages like this, we see how the scriptures view past events as patterns for understanding the present. The New Testament invokes the same process when it presents various phases in Jesus' life as "according to the scriptures," especially the culmination of Jesus' life as a passover-exodus-entry into the promised land.

Psalm 126:1-2, 2-3, 4-5, 6

The people are deeply disturbed, threatened by misfortune. Our meditation includes the whole psalm, divided into two sections. In vv. 1-3, we join Israel to recall the hopes and the joys once ours. In vv. 4-6, we pray that our former good fortune be restored. Though we are planting in tears, may we reap in gladness. Our hope is based on past experience, as expressed in the community response: "The Lord has done great things for us: we are filled with joy."

Philippians 3:8-14

Paul's former Jewish ideals had called forth a zealous, irreproachable response from him (3:4-7). Now that he knew Christ, all else, including his Jewish origins, appeared insignificant (v. 8). He had been a just man under the law (v. 6). Now the only justice he holds precious comes through faith in Christ (v. 9, cf. Philippians 3:17-4:1, p. 46). Paul's uprightness before God and people is based on his personal relationship with Christ.

To appreciate Paul's statement, we must view faith as a developing

personal knowledge in which the parties freely reach out to one another. In
the relationship, God has the initiative. What he shares is his personal
self. To accept God's self-gift, we must reciprocate by opening our person
to God. Faith is a communion with God, a life relationship, not an abstract
knowledge or a set of formulas to be believed. Formulas are based on faith
experience but cannot be equated with it. Faith's object is a person, not a
statement. As Paul says, his faith is "in Christ" (v. 9).

In light of this understanding of faith, Paul's effort to develop in his
knowledge of Christ and to resemble him even in the resurrection becomes
quite comprehensible (vv. 10-11). Of its nature faith is a process. The
remaining verses describe Paul as on the way and indicate the strong
influence of the goal on his present efforts. The apostle's athletic imagery
remains effective today (vv. 12-14).

John 8:1-11

The Johannine authenticity of this story is doubtful but the church
accepts it as an integral part of the New Testament. It is an excellent
example of Jesus' general teaching not to judge others. From a literary
point of view, the unit's attitude toward the sinner and repentance is
closely related to Luke.

The passage attests the harsh judgmental manner of many of Jesus'
contemporaries and the public humiliation to which sinners were exposed
(v. 3). The incident takes place in the temple while Jesus is teaching (v. 2).
A woman surprised in adultery is used by Pharisees to trap Jesus on a point
of law. In view of this (vv. 5-6), we must assume Jesus had a reputation for
mercy to sinners and his manner of dealing with them was judged by many
as out of keeping with the prescriptions of Mosaic law.

Jesus' response presents him as gentle and forgiving toward the woman
(vv. 10-11) and extremely clever at avoiding the trap. Refusing to respond
directly, he asks the person with no sin to cast the first stone (v. 7). The law
is not the real issue here, but the self-righteous, dishonest attitude of the
woman's accusers. Elsewhere in the gospel traditions, Jesus is equally
adept at avoiding the legal traps set by his enemies.

> *1. In our search for understanding how God is active in the
> disorienting realities of the present, we should seek biblical
> precedents, but we must also be open to the new and unexpected
> (Isaiah 43:16-21).*

> *2. The distinction between faith and its formulation is fun-*

damental for us who take both tradition and new developments seriously (Philippians 3:8-14).

3. How do we view ourselves, how do outsiders know us? A church noted for judgmental severity or for love and humble forgiveness (John 8:1-11)?

Passion (Palm) Sunday

Jesus' passion and death were extremely disorienting for the first followers who had placed their hope for salvation in him. In light of the resurrection, however, they came to discover its significance and articulated it in terms of Jesus' attitudes (Luke 22:14-23:56) and Isaiah's servant songs (Isaiah 50:4-7). In a theology of God's eternal providence, Jesus' willing and humble acceptance of humanity to the point of death moved God to exalt him. His new life calls for universal recognition of his lordship (Philippians 2:6-11).

Isaiah 50:4-7

Deutero-Isaiah includes four oracular poems called the "song of the suffering servant" (42:1-4; 49:1-7; 50:4-9; 52:13-53:12). These hymns strongly affirm the purposefulness of human suffering. New Testament tradition turned to them to find the significance of Jesus' sufferings according to the scriptures. The early Christians discovered a biblical pattern that gave meaning to Christ's sufferings in line with earlier expressions of God's presence to his people.

This third servant song sings of the persecution willingly accepted by God's servant in fulfillment of his vocation. The servant knows God has given him the ability to listen deeply and truly, and the verbal facility to rouse the weary (v. 4). What he hears, harsh though it is, has not deterred him from his prophetic role as God's spokesman (v. 5). He courageously accepted the insults and abuse of his hearers (v. 6), without disgrace or shame because God was with him (v. 7). This strength and hope pervade the rest of the hymn (vv. 8-9).

Psalm 22:8-9, 17-18, 19-20, 23-24

Psalm 22 contributed forcefully to the Christian telling of Jesus' passion. Verses 8-9, 17-18, 19 express the anguish of his suffering, while vv. 20,

They shall mount up with wings as eagles.

23-24 formulate his prayer and grateful response to God's salvific act. The assembly's cry, "My God, my God, why have you abandoned me?" (v. 2), is set in the context of suffering's orientation to glory.

Philippians 2:6-11

Paul has slightly modified an early Christological hymn and inserted it into his text. Because it portrayed Christ's attitude, the hymn gave him a model for the Christian's humble, selfless attention to others' interests (2:1-5). Paul added the phrases "death on a cross" (v. 8), "to the glory of God the Father" (v. 11), and possibly "in the heavens, on the earth and under the earth" (v. 10).

The hymn is clearly divided into two parts, each composed of a lengthy sentence in the Greek. In vv. 6-8, Christ is the subject; in vv. 9-11, he is the object. What Christ does is the reason for what God does in his behalf. Christ thoroughly empties or humbles himself, and accepts the ultimate consequence of the human condition, death (vv. 6-8); *therefore*, God exalted him (vv. 9-11). The slave (v. 7) has become Lord (v. 11).

Luke 22:14-23:56

One of the remarkable things about the gospel tradition is that the passion of Jesus did not slip into oblivion when the Christians came to new hope after his resurrection. We would think they would have been only too happy to forget a bad episode in Jesus' career and focus on his glorious risen life and the happier days of his historical life. That they did not do so is a strong witness to the realism embedded in our Christian origins.

For Jesus, in glory, the passion was indeed over. His followers, however, had yet to earn their share in Christ's glory. Pain and suffering were very much realities of the present. By reflecting on Jesus' passion, his followers squarely faced the reality of human suffering. Christ had shown suffering led to glory. This was not a morbid, masochistic or despairing exercise. Told by followers who rejoiced in Christ's resurrection, the passion is a hopeful story about suffering that at first appeared meaningless but now stood meaning-filled. At no point does the account prescind from Christ's glory.

Each of the four New Testament accounts is different, reflecting the literary and theological intentions of its author. In Luke's account, composure and tremendous dignity characterize Jesus throughout the passion. The important Lukan theme of salvation for the repentant sinner is woven into the story of those crucified with Jesus (23:32-33, 39-43). To appreciate what Luke has accomplished at this point, compare his account with Mark 15:27-32 and Matthew 27:44, where repentance and salvation are absent. The author also goes to considerable length to show Jesus was innocent, recognized as such by Roman officials (cf. 23:4, 14, 15, 22). These observations help us appreciate the distinctive approach taken by each evangelist.

1. Present sufferings do have meaning, even if we cannot discern it. A biblical perspective should help us to trust unflinchingly (Isaiah 50:4-7).

2. Jesus' absolute acceptance of the human condition (including death) resulted in God's exalting him to new life (Philippians 2:6-11).

3. Jesus has entered into glory, but reflection on his passion still has value for us (Luke 22:14-23:56).

Easter

Easter

The season begins with Easter, develops through six Sundays and climaxes on Pentecost. The Thursday between the sixth and seventh Sundays is a special celebration of Jesus' ascension.

Like the Christmas season, which complements the season of Advent, Easter crowns the efforts and fulfills the hopes of Lent. Lent presupposes Easter, and the celebration of the resurrection is inseparable from that of the passion. Lent presented the gospel from the point of view of Christ's passion and suffering and the Christian response to sin and evil. The Easter synthesis of the gospel views the Christian mystery in its fulfillment and presents the values that lead to glory.

Our Easter celebration begins with visits to Jesus' tomb. The tomb, symbol of despair, becomes one of hope as life is boldly affirmed in the face of death (John 20:1-9). The season climaxes with Pentecost, an infusion of the risen Lord's energies into the community's apostolic life (John 20:19-23). Life is lifeless unless it is shared.

The resurrection is not a restoration of Jesus' historical life, but a total transformation into new life in God. In the mystery of Jesus' ascension, the community is charged to continue Jesus' work in history (Luke 24:46-53). The Spirit-filled community gives historical, sacramental expression to the risen Lord's life.

From the second to the seventh Sundays of Easter, we focus on the various aspects of Christian life that lead to its promised fulfillment. With John's gospel, we reflect on faith (20:19-31), love (21:1-19), obedience (10:27-30), the new commandment (John 13:31-33, 34-35), openness to the Spirit (14:23-29), and trust in Christ's prayer for the church in every age (17:20-26). We draw inspiration from the life of the early Christian community as presented in Acts and from Revelation's vision of the church's ultimate fulfillment.

Easter Sunday

On Easter, we turn from the tomb to focus on the person of the risen Lord (John 20:1-9). We are witnesses because of our eucharistic experience at the Lord's table. Therefore, we must proclaim the resurrection gospel (Acts 10:34, 37-43). With him who transcends history, we learn to cope with the ambiguities and tensions of the committed life (Colossians 3:1-4 or 1 Corinthians 5:6-8).

Acts 10:34, 37-43

Acts focuses on the mission to the gentiles. Peter's discourse to Cornelius' Caesarea household is a major turning point in the narrative. Verses 35-36 (omitted from the *Lectionary*) present the context: God's impartiality (v. 34b) requires a gospel open to all, not limited to Israel (cf. Acts 10:34-38).

But the liturgy prescinds from this context and concentrates on Peter's message about Jesus' career (vv. 37-40a), about God's deeds on his behalf (vv. 40b-41), about Jesus' work through commissioned witnesses (v. 42), and about the testimony of Old Testament prophets (v. 43).

The text is a summary of early apostolic preaching. We find similar examples in the discourses of Peter and Paul, as well as in other parts of Luke-Acts. Independent of any application, the central message was that God raised Jesus from the dead.

An extraordinary point is that Christ's witnesses are those who ate and drank with him after he rose from the dead. Christ was viewed as a participant at the eucharistic meal, only secondarily or indirectly as nourishment. As participant, Christ was present at post-Easter meals through those gathered in the assembly.

Psalm 118:1-2, 16-17, 22-23

In Psalm 118, we give thanks to the Lord and proclaim his everlasting mercy (vv. 1-2). With the psalmist, we shout our appreciation of God's power, singing of life's victory over death (vv. 16-17). God has taken the rejected one and made him the foundation of our Christian edifice (vv. 22-23). To these appropriately paschal lines the assembly responds, "This is the day the Lord has made; let us rejoice and be glad." The liturgy views the Easter events as the supreme manifestation of God's wonderful works (v. 23).

Colossians 3:1-4

In a lengthy concluding section (3:1—4:6), Paul exhorts his readers to reach for the ideal of Christian life as they exercise their various roles in the world. The introduction (3:1-4) describes the basis of this life: Christians have died with Christ (v. 2) and have been raised up in his company (v. 1). Paul is referring to the readers' baptismal initiation.

Although Christians share in Christ's risen life, that life has yet to be fully manifested. When Christ finally does appear, Christians will appear with him in glorious fulfillment of their present life. Paul comes to grips with the tension between our present relation to the risen Lord and our currently unglorified state.

This distinction between the hidden risen life and its future revelation is the key to Paul's Christian ethics. In the present, Christians keep their attention on the higher things in store for them. This attitude will sustain them in their Christian living.

1 Corinthians 5:6-8

Paul is rebuking the Corinthian community about a specific case of immorality, and the leaven metaphor is central to these verses. Jewish religious practice excluded leaven from the new bread used for Passover and the Feast of the Unleavened Bread. The exclusion signified gratitude for the new harvest.

Paul first gives us a general principle in question form. Just as leaven affects an entire loaf, a whole community is influenced by problems and members' attitudes toward them (v. 6b). Second, Paul issues a command to remove all the old leaven—that is, their former unredeemed way of life—so they may be truly unleavened as Christ's Passover had made them (v. 7). Finally, Christians celebrate Christ's Passover by putting aside malice and evil (the old leaven) and taking up the sincerity and truth their new state calls for (v. 8).

John 20:1-9

Stories of visits to Jesus' tomb on the first day of the week are deeply rooted in Christian tradition. Their most extensive development is in John's gospel (20:1-18). In general, the literary and pastoral purpose is to proclaim the resurrection of Jesus of Nazareth. Accordingly, every line vibrates with Easter faith and joy.

Today's reading includes two distinct episodes, Mary Magdalen's visit

(vv. 1-2) and that of Peter and the other disciple, the one Jesus loved (vv. 3-9). Mary Magdalen figures in all the gospels' accounts of the women's visit.

We may think of the empty tomb as proof of Jesus' resurrection, but it raised no such faith in Mary. Seeing the tomb open (v. 1), she ran away and reported the matter as a problem (v. 2). Only with a recognition experience of the risen Lord does she come to Easter faith (vv. 11-18).

Once it was known in faith that Jesus was living and glorious, the empty tomb became a marvelous historical and literary symbol of the resurrection. Before that, it stood for Jesus' death.

The Peter and John story (vv. 3-10) indicates that, with time, the empty tomb replaced the actual appearances of Jesus as the experiential ground for faith in his resurrection. This proved inadequate, however, because we see theological interest shift from the tomb to Jesus' burial wrappings (vv. 6-7).

We live 19 centuries after these events, but the gospel text and the traditional stories of the empty tomb can still clarify and articulate our experience of the risen Lord. We must never forget that the texts presuppose an experience. In any historical context, an empty tomb *by itself* is at best an ambiguous sign.

> *1. Christ the risen Lord is present in the participants at the eucharistic table, sharing his person with all open to his presence (Acts 10:42).*
>
> *2. Our share in Christ's risen life has begun. Its eventual fullness should encourage us as we assume our Christian responsibilities (Colossians 3:1-4).*
>
> *3. Faith in the risen Lord rests on a divinely inspired experience of his living presence, not on indirect human "proofs" (John 20:1-9).*

Second Sunday of Easter

Easter faith is grounded in the risen Lord's communication of peace in and through the Christian assembly. We join the early Christians and Thomas to affirm our faith in Christ, the living manifestation of God's lordship and divinity (John 20:19-31). God's signs and wonders punctuate our communal

*sharing as they once did through the apostles (Acts 5:12-16). A
reading from the book of Revelation (1:9-11, 12-13, 17-19) helps
us appreciate the transcendent quality of our liturgical and
apostolic experiences.*

Acts 5:12-16

Luke's account of the beginnings of the Easter community at Jerusalem
includes three major summaries of its life and ideals. The first (2:42-47)
encompasses the whole range of the community's attitudes and activities.
The second (4:32-35) focuses on a main element, the communal sharing of
goods (2:42, 44-45). The third (5:12-16) develops the signs and wonders the
apostles wrought during their daily visits to the temple (2:43, 46) and the
growing popular response to their activity (2:47).

The expression "signs and wonders" (5:12; 2:43) evokes the great divine
manifestations that accompanied Israel's exodus from Egypt. In the Old
Testament, the phrase appears mainly in Jeremiah and Deuteronomy, in a
theological effort to show that God's covenant relationship to Israel cannot be relegated to past history. The covenant and God's saving acts are
now. In Acts, that "now" is reaffirmed in relation to the church's life.
God's work on our behalf did not end with Jesus' death-resurrection. It
continued in the life of the apostolic community. It was manifested in
those who joined the earliest witnesses and inherited their missionary
responsibility.

The main expression of these signs and wonders lay in healing, an
important part of Jesus' mission, which Luke emphasized in his first
volume. The author wants to show the essential continuity between Jesus'
mission and the church's.

The Old and New Testaments did not distinguish between physical and
spiritual healing. In fact, physical ailments and their cures were seen as
signs of God's all-encompassing regard for his people. Consequently, we
should not interpret them in a fundamentalist fashion. Our challenge is to
view human ailments as signs of the deeper sickness afflicting those who
wander far from God. The physician's cure is part of the broader healing
the church is called to perform in its work of reconciliation.

Psalm 118:2-4, 13-15, 22-24

In verses from a psalm of thanksgiving for deliverance from distress, the
liturgy calls forth universal gratitude. God's loving mercy is without end
(vv. 2-4). We have witnessed it in the struggle when God came to our aid

(vv. 13-15). We found ourselves rejected, but we have been selected for an eminent position (vv. 22-24). The community responds, "Give thanks to the Lord for he is good, his love is everlasting."

Revelation 1:9-11, 12-13, 17-19

This introductory vision (1:9-20) commissions a writer to transmit letters (2:1-3:22) to seven churches in the province of Asia (western Turkey). After introducing the author (v. 9), the narrative presents a heavenly message (vv. 10-11), a vision (vv. 12-13, 14-16), the visionary's reaction (v. 17a) and a heavenly response (v. 17b-19). The unit ends with an interpretation of two important symbols (v. 20).

The passage is full of surrealistic symbols, drawn from the Old Testament or early Christian tradition. They are not photographic images of the divine but impressions of the transcendent. The divine eludes our conceptual and imaginative abilities. In the older apocalyptic literature this language referred to events in the future. In the present context it describes the relationship between heavenly realities and the earthly events of actual human experience.

Basically, the unit is patterned on Daniel 10, enriched with symbolic language from Daniel 7, Exodus and Ezekiel. Symbols with no biblical or early Christian antecedent (the seven stars and lampstands) are explained in v. 20. The author wants to clarify elements outside the reader's religious culture.

Two important terms deserve special consideration: the Son of Man and the Lord's Day. "One like a Son of Man" (v. 13) evokes Daniel 7:13 and many passages in the gospel tradition. In Daniel, the term Son of Man refers to the end of time. In the gospel passages, it describes the Lord's presence to Christians who must, like him, endure suffering to enter into kingly glory (v. 9). The "Lord's Day" (v. 10) evokes God's definitive intervention already inaugurated by Christ's resurrection, but it refers directly to its celebration on Sunday, the Lord's liturgical day.

John 20:19-31

The reading includes three short literary units, each with ample material for a Sunday homily!

First we have an appearance of Jesus to a group of disciples (vv. 19-23). The time is evening of the week's first day, on which Jesus' tomb had been discovered empty. The fact that Jesus appeared to Thomas exactly one week later when the community had again assembled (v. 26) indicates that

Sunday had already become a Christian day of the Lord. The characteristic greeting of the risen Lord to his followers is "Peace be with you" (vv. 19, 21, 26), a liturgical greeting rich in biblical and early Christian tradition. Coming from the risen Lord, it expresses the new covenant's benefits.

The second unit is the well-known story of Thomas (vv. 24-29). The opening lines (vv. 24-25) are situated during the week between the two Sunday assemblies. They link verses 26-29 with the first appearance and raise the important question of the ground of belief in the risen Lord. The main part sees Thomas come to faith during the assembly. Two points are emphasized. First, although the risen Lord has a mode of being unrelated to time and space (v. 26), he is the same person who died on the cross (v. 27). Second, with or without seeing, faith is absolutely required to confess God's presence in the risen Lord (vv. 28-29). At one time, emphasis may have been on the reality of the risen Lord. In John's gospel, however, the significance of the risen Lord had to be clarified. John wants to show the possibility of belief for those who had not shared in the early experience of the post-Easter community.

The third unit is the evangelist's concluding statement (vv. 30-31). The author indicates his intention in writing this gospel.

1. Christians must discover the signs of God's marvelous saving actions in everyday human life (Acts 5:12-16).

2. As Christians we continue to give historical expression to the life and mission of Jesus whose history ended when he entered into glory (Acts 5:12-16).

3. The characteristic greeting of the risen Lord, "Peace be with you," is the fundamental attitude of those who share his life (John 20:19-23).

Third Sunday of Easter

Christ's communication of his risen person in the eucharist calls for a steadfast, loving response. That communication is a celebration of our apostolic work. It gradually penetrates love's surface expressions to evoke a deep, realistic commitment (John 21:1-19). That commitment sustains us when we meet resistance and persecution (Acts 5:27-32, 40-41), which must be seen in the context of Christ's final manifestation (Revelation 5:11-14).

*Liturgically, Christ's passion-resurrection illumines our lives
in Christian history.*

Acts 5:27-32, 40-41

The book of Acts is a sequel to the gospels. Like them, it is a story of
persecution and hope, an account of courage and freedom in an environ-
ment of constraint. In today's first reading, we find the apostolic community led before Jerusalem's religious governing body (the Sanhedrin) for
interrogation.

After a short introductory statement (v. 27), the high priest reproaches
the apostles for teaching about Christ's name and accuses them of trying to
make the Sanhedrin responsible for Christ's death (v. 28). The grounds for
this accusation lay in the proclamation of Jesus' death-resurrection, which
placed Jewish leaders in an unfavorable light. Its motivation sprang from
the Christian community's rapid growth and the consequent threat to the
Sanhedrin's authoritative position before the people.

Peter and the apostles respond by reaffirming the value of their witness
(v. 32a). For them it was a matter of obedience, that is, of responding with
practical faith to God's revelation in history (vv. 29, 32b). In New Testament times, the term *obedience* was broader than in present-day usage.

Concretely, God had responded to the crucifixion by raising Jesus to
glory. Far from condemnatory, this action was an invitation to repentance
and an offer of forgiveness (vv. 30-31). Likewise, when the apostles
preached Jesus as ruler and savior, their purpose was not to condemn
anyone, even Jesus' accusers, but to extend his forgiveness to them. If the
Sanhedrin repented, it would no longer find itself threatened. The discourse is both a defense of the apostles' preaching and an expression of
pastoral concern for their interrogators.

Chapter 5:40-41 describes the Sanhedrin's reaction to Gamaliel's speech
(5:35-39), omitted from today's reading.

Psalm 30:2, 4, 5-6, 11-13

God has saved us from death. We sing his praises with verses from a
thanksgiving psalm (vv. 2, 4) and invite the faithful to do the same. The
night's weeping gives way to rejoicing (vv. 5-6). Our meditation ends with
a prayer for the loving mercy God has shown in the past. We are confident
and pledge unending gratitude (vv. 11-13). The psalm is summarized in the
community's response: "I will praise you, Lord, for you have rescued me."

Revelation 5:11-14

The reading is the conclusion of the second comissioning vision (4:1-5:14) in the book of Revelation. Unlike the first vision (see p. 66), it refers to history's climactic moment (4:1), when Jesus Christ (1:5), the One like a Son of Man (1:13) and the Lamb who had been slain (5:6), will come in judgment to receive divine honors from the heavenly court in full assembly. On that day the faithful will join the angels in praising God (4:8-11) and Christ (5:11-14), who in his paschal sacrifice had created a royal, worshiping people for God (5:9-10).

The author evokes a scene in sharp contrast with present historical conditions. The forces of evil are at war with the Christian movement and all seems contrary to the promise of glory heralded by Christ's resurrection. By presenting the final outcome of this struggle, the second vision gives encouragement to remain faithful in persecution and extends a powerful word of hope to all who suffer.

The passage describes a scene of worship, and the language is quite appropriately drawn from Old Testament passages assumed into early Christian worship as well as from specifically Christian liturgical traditions.

The doxology in v. 12, addressed to the Lamb, is a continuation of a hymn of praise sung to God himself (4:11). The grounds for this link, between divine worship and worship of the Lamb once slain but now standing glorious, is given in 5:9-10 where the Lamb's former historical action in establishing God's kingdom had already been extolled in a new song. The introduction to v. 13 recalls the hymn quoted in Philippians 2:6-11 (cf. v. 10), and its doxology echoes Psalm 150:6.

John 21:1-19

The reading includes an appearance to seven disciples (v. 2) at the Sea of Tiberias (vv. 1-14), followed by the first part of a dialogue (vv. 15-23) between the risen Christ and Simon Peter. The narrative forms the major portion of an appendix written either by the major Johannine author or a close associate. Unlike the gospel appearances (chapter 20) which were situated in Jerusalem (cf. also Luke 24), the geographical setting for the Johannine appendix is the shore of the Sea of Tiberias in Galilee (cf. Matthew 28:16-20).

The appearance story (vv. 1-14) is a meal narrative strong in eucharistic allusions (v. 13). The risen Lord is experienced in the eucharistic assembly, the point of departure for the Christian mission. Literarily, the latter theme has been integrated into the meal context by means of a tradition concerning a miraculous catch of fish (cf. Luke 5:4-11). This story, whose implications were basically ecclesiological (cf. Mark 1:17), could have been placed either in the historical life of Jesus or in the resurrection narratives, because both settings have significance for the life of the Christian communities.

The dialogue with Peter includes a triple question and answer bearing on the apostle's mission. In place of fish, the ecclesiological metaphor is now sheep, a theme with Old Testament antecedents, widely developed in many parts of the New including John. Jesus' threefold questioning recalls Peter's triple denial. In light of John 13:37 and Mark 14:29, note the humility with which Peter now professes his love for Christ.

> *1. The proclamation of the resurrection in word and deed should be presented as a gesture of reconciliation for those open to life's fullness (Acts 5:37-42).*
>
> *2. Does our eucharist favor a personal and communal faith experience of the risen Lord and provide a stimulus for the Christian mission (John 21:1-14)?*
>
> *3. What must be the attitude of leaders in Christ's church (John 21:15-19)?*

Fourth Sunday of Easter

Christian discipleship is the way to eternal life. John 10:27-30 presents life in Christ's flock in light of its term, when we shall join our shepherd in his union with the Father. To achieve that union, we must accept the gospel as God's word to all. Exclusiveness betrays the gospel and can lead to our exclusion from the community of salvation (Acts 13:14, 43-52). Revelation 7:9, 14-17 shows the glory awaiting those who stand true in their commitment to the end.

Acts 13:14, 43-52

The reading is from Luke's account of the first mission from Antioch (13:1-14:28). It includes a verse (13:14) from the introduction (13:13-15) to Paul's long discourse at Antioch in Pisidia (13:16-41) as well as the events after Paul's synagogue address.

Verse 14 provides a synagogal setting for Paul and Barnabas' initial activities. With v. 43, we accompany the assembly out of the synagogue to witness the Jews' first response to Paul's presentation of the basic Christian message. The situation resembles the favorable response that first greeted Jesus' self-presentation in the Nazareth synagogue (Luke 4:22). However, once Paul takes his message into the streets and addresses gentiles, who respond enthusiastically, the Jews' positive reaction becomes negative and increasingly violent (14:44-45). Their second response parallels the negative attitude toward Jesus' challenging announcement of a mission to the gentiles (Luke 4:28-30).

Paul presents the immediate historical basis for the gentile mission. Since the apostolic message was rejected by the Jews, the gospel would be announced to the gentiles (14:46). He develops the biblical basis for this mission (14:47) and confirms the gentiles in their openness to the gospel (14:48). The previously unforeseen is situated in the context of biblical revelation and presented as the providential unfolding of a divine plan.

Psalm 100: 1-2, 3, 5

Our meditative psalm includes all but v. 4 of this hymn of praise, a concluding doxology for a collection of royal psalms (Psalms 93, 95-99). We begin with a call to joyful song, glad service and entry into the Lord's royal presence (vv. 1-2). This call and its response are based on God's relationship to us as creator and Lord of history (v. 3). We conclude by extolling the Lord's enduring goodness and faithfulness (v. 5). In the metaphorical language of v. 3, the community sings: "We are his people: the sheep of his flock."

Revelation 7:9, 11-17

After the inaugural vision and the liturgical manifestation of chapters 4 and 5 (see p. 69), the author presents Christ as presiding over history's close by opening a perfectly sealed (seven seals) scroll (6:1-8:1). It reveals the mystery of God's immutable will for the end of time (1:19). Today's reading forms part of an interruption (7:1-17) between the opening of the sixth (6:12-17) and the seventh (8:1) seals. This interpolation contrasts the glorious position of the faithful with the fearful condition of the ungodly (6:15-17) when Christ comes in judgment.

The first part of the vision describes God's protection of the church on earth (7:1-8); the second part describes the church in heaven standing before the throne of the Lamb and glorifying God (7:9-17). The vast assembly of the heavenly church is presented in an attitude of worship (v. 9).

Passing over the initial expressions of praise, in which the church is associated with the angels (vv. 10-13), the reading identifies those present as the Christians who have survived the great period of trial (v. 14a). With this vision of future glory, the author encourages his readers to stand faithful in their present trials. He reminds them their suffering associates them with the sacrifice of the Lamb (v. 14b). This encouragement is reinforced by a magnificent statement, poetic and biblically inspired. It evokes the theological grandeur of Christian liturgy and the paradisiac state of those who will enjoy its ultimate fulfillment (vv. 15-17).

John 10:27-30

The time is the feast of the Dedication, a celebration of the temple's rededication by the Maccabees (164 B.C.) after its desecration by Antiochus IV Epiphanes (167 B.C.). We know this feast by its Hebrew name, Hanukkah. As Jesus was walking in Solomon's Portico, along the east side of the vast temple area, he was confronted by the Jews: if he is the messiah, let him say so clearly (10:22-24).

At first reading, Jesus seems to refuse them an answer. He explains why no answer would be adequate for them. To recognize him as messiah, the Jews would have to believe in him and be his disciples, which was far from the case (10:25-26). Today's reading begins when Jesus contrasts his disciples with the crowd. He resumes the metaphor of sheep and shepherd (v. 27) that had dominated chapter 10:1-18. Like spouse, kingdom, son and their correlatives, this metaphor transposed the older legal terminology of Israel's covenant with God into terms closer to Jewish and Christian experience. In this the New Testament continued a religious tradition that originated especially in early prophetic literature.

Jesus' sheep hear, that is, recognize and heed, his voice and follow him. The pasture to which Jesus leads them is eternal life where no one can perish (v. 28), because the Father himself has given Jesus his flock. In their work of shepherding Jesus and the Father are absolutely united (v. 30). Jesus' message challenges all who continue the mission the Father had given him (17:18; 21:21).

> *1. Like the early Christians, we must situate unforeseen events in the continuum of biblical history. We can discover meaning in historical changes that at first appear meaningless (Acts 13:43-52).*

2. For Christians, suffering has positive value in relation to Christ's suffering which led to glory (Revelation 7:14-17).

3. Christians understand who Christ really is by believing in him and assuming the challenge of discipleship (John 10:27-30).

Fifth Sunday of Easter

Christian love is the historical sign of Christ's love after his glorious departure from history. Today's gospel presents the new commandment of love and juxtaposes its challenge with Judas' rejection (John 13:31-33, 34-35). The church leaders or presbyters must help the community remain faithful in that love through trials (Acts 14:21-27). Love is creative: the new commandment leads to eternal life (Revelation 21:1-5).

Acts 14:21-27

The reading describes the apostolic journey from Derbe to Antioch on the Orontes, cradle of the Pauline missions. The itinerary in 14:21, 24-26 retraces in reverse the course that had brought Paul and Barnabas to Perga and Pamphilia (13:13), Antioch in Pisidia (13:14), Iconium (13:51), Lystra (14:6) and Derbe (14:20). Worthy of special note are an apostolic instruction to the disciples (v. 22) and the installation of presbyters (v. 23).

After the departure of Paul and Barnabas from Pisidian Antioch (see p. 70), the community needed reassurance and encouragement. The apostles responded by emphasizing the necessity of trials if Christians are to enter God's reign (14:22). Luke recalls the historical circumstances that surrounded the early Pauline missions but, more importantly, he reveals a serious problem for the post-apostolic church. In his estimation, Paul's message remained extremely relevant for the gentile churches of the 80's. According to scripture, suffering is the way to the kingdom, a pattern established by Jesus' death-resurrection.

Before leaving Pisidian Antioch, Paul and Barnabas installed a group of elders or presbyters, men to guide the local church in the absence of its itinerant founders. They prepared for service by joining the apostles in prayer and fasting. Elders played a significant role in Jewish communities and they continued that role when these communities became Christian. The gentile communities were organized along lines that sprang from the social structure of Jewish life. Later these elders would take on many of the roles and functions of the order of presbyters. They constitute an important link in the history of the priesthood as we now know it.

Psalm 145: 8-9, 10-11, 12-13

Psalm 145 is a hymn of praise extolling the qualities of Israel's God. He is good, merciful, slow to anger and kind. These qualities affect all his relationships (vv. 8-9). They also call for universal gratitude and blessing as we tell the story of his mighty deeds (vv. 10-11). All must know of God's royal dominion (vv. 12-13). Accordingly, the community responds: "I will praise your name forever, my king and my God."

Revelation 21:1-5

The vision of the new creation (21:1-22:5) is the literary climax of the book of Revelation. As the sequel to the final judgment (21:11-15), it involves the transformation of all earthly realities into a world suited to the glorious condition of the saved. It is the fulfillment of the divine intervention initiated by Jesus' death-resurrection. Today's reading includes the introduction to this vision (vv. 1-4) and the opening statement (v. 5) of its development.

The reference to the new heaven and the new earth, and many of the unit's other elements, are reminiscent of Isaiah 65:17-19 and 66:22. Although God has in store a new creation, it stands in continuity with the old. Consequently, though our present world is a place of struggle and difficulty, it cannot be seen as radically evil.

The sea disappears because it has no counterpart in the new creation. Ancient interpretations saw the sea as the netherworld or place of death (Jonah 2), a primeval chaos (Genesis 1:1-2) that threatened to destroy the order of the first creation (Genesis 6-9).

Jerusalem, which had been destroyed, is recreated as the new abode of God's presence (vv. 2-3a). The ancient covenant of mutual presence between God and people (v. 3b) is fulfilled, forever assured as a covenant of peace and happiness (v. 4).

Finally, God summarizes the entire action in one brief statement about the newness of all things. He orders the author to write the vision to encourage those whose lives are still enmeshed in history's struggle. Present events notwithstanding, God's words are trustworthy and true (v. 5).

John 13:31-33, 34-35

With chapter 13 we begin the second part of John's gospel (chapters 13-20). This "book of glory," as it is frequently called, includes a long prelude (chapter 13), Jesus' farewell discourse (chapters 14-17), and the passion-glorification narrative (chapters 18-20). Today's reading is the second of two short discourses inserted in the prelude. The first (13:12-20) follows Jesus' washing of the disciples' feet (13:1-11). It announces the passion. The second (13:31-35) follows the account of Judas' betrayal (13:21-30). It announces Jesus' glorification. The prelude concludes with Jesus' prediction of Peter's betrayal (13:36-38), an immediate transition to the long discourse and the narrative of the passion-glorification.

Like Jesus' farewell discourse, the prefatory discourses set Jesus' in the context of a last meal with his disciples. All three discourses provide Jesus with an opportunity to address future generations concerning the way of life and the attitudes implied by his passion-glorification. Full of love and light, Jesus' attitude contrasts sharply with the dark night of Judas' betrayal (13:30).

Once Judas has left the master's table, Jesus speaks (13:31a). The discourse is divided into two parts. First, Jesus instructs his disciples on the glory he is about to enter. He must leave his "children" (vv. 31-33). Second, he gives them a new commandment (vv. 34-35). Jesus' followers must have love for one another (v. 34a). Modeled on Jesus' love (v. 34b), the disciples' love is a sign they are indeed his disciples (v. 35). Jesus' commandment is in direct continuity with Old Testament attitudes. It is new, however, in its Christian inspiration, as an expression of the new relationships that bind Jesus' followers in a new covenant. Reborn in a new community, the disciples enjoy a new fellowship that provides a distinctive point of departure for Christian love.

1. Christian leaders are drawn from the community and prepared for their role of service by prayer and fasting (Acts 14:23).

2. The acceptance of our Christian responsibility to extend Christ's work in history presupposes we have come to terms with his departure. We do not spend our time trying to restore a time which is past (John 13:31-33).

3. Christian love is the sign of true disciples, a sacramental expression of God's love for people (John 13:34-35).

Sixth Sunday of Easter

We must constantly recall Jesus' word if it is to illumine the new historical situations through which we develop as a church. In John 14:23-29, we see our efforts as the Spirit's gift, helping us to transcend the limitations of earlier stages in our history (Acts 15:1-2, 22-29). When all limitations are finally overcome, we shall live in the new Jerusalem, where God will be present in the assembly of the saved. No longer will he need a special dwelling place (Revelation 21:10-14, 22-23).

Acts 15:1-2, 22-29

In Luke's time, the Christian community at Antioch had long replaced Jerusalem as the center of eastern Christianity. Today's reading dwells on a special problem in the early years of Antiochene Christianity. It shows how the community referred to Jerusalem in its effort to resolve basic questions, and demonstrates how the mother community of all churches responded to the Antioch situation.

The question that led to an apostolic assembly at Jerusalem was the necessity of circumcision for gentiles (15:1-2). This problem was a symbol for the much deeper issue of the church's universality. The church was a new phenomenon and its life represented a new era in biblical history. But did it actually transcend ancient Israel and its institutions, or merely open Israel's doors to universal membership?

A decision for transcendence would mean the church could develop among gentiles without concern for Jewish life. Gentiles would not need circumcision or the practice of Jewish law and custom. On the other hand, if the church was only the universalization of Judaism, gentiles would first have to become Jews to be Christians. The church would be defined as a Jewish reality open to gentile proselytes.

Jerusalem responded by affirming the radical transcendence of Christianity, requiring gentile communities to avoid only those practices that appeared illicit for all Christians independently of their cultural and religious origins (15:22-29). Luke's presentation of the problem and its resolution corresponds substantially with what we know from the Pauline letters. It challenges our church to transcend its Western roots as it proclaims the gospel to peoples whose history remained independent of ours until the colonial expansion of the West.

Psalm 67: 2-3, 5, 6 and 8

A bounteous harvest occasions this thanksgiving psalm. May God continue to bless us, may his goodness be known to all nations (vv. 2-3). The nations are called to rejoice with Israel and join in divine praise (vv. 5-6, 8). This universalist attitude is reflected in the assembly's response: "O God, let all the nations praise you!"

Revelation 21:10-14, 22-23

Today's second reading provides further elements from Revelation's description of the new creation (see p. 74). Attention centers on the new Jerusalem introduced in 21:2-4. The text includes the first section (21:10-14) of an elaborate presentation (21:10-21), an extremely important reflection on the absence of a temple in the heavenly Jerusalem (v. 22), and a comment on the new city's source of light (v. 23).

Most of the symbols and images describing the new Jerusalem were drawn from Ezekiel 40-48. In Ezekiel, however, the main emphasis had been on the city's new temple. For the author of Revelation, Christ is the new temple, the perfect place of God's dwelling. Since Christ is present throughout the church, not restricted to any particular part of it, it makes no sense to speak of a temple within the new Jerusalem. The temple is coextensive with the church which is the new Jerusalem.

The sun and the moon stand outside the new creation. God's glory supplies light; and Christ the Lamb, in whom the divine glory is reflected, is the light of the new Jerusalem. This is the author's vision of the church arrived at Christ's fullness.

John 14:23-29

The passage is from Jesus' farewell discourse. In 14:17-21, he had indicated he would manifest himself to his disciples but not to the world, that is, those who cannot recognize the Spirit of truth (v. 17). The disciples, however, had anticipated a general public manifestation. In their name, Judas (not Iscariot) asks why Jesus would limit his self-revelation to his circle of disciples (14:22). Jesus responds by focusing the community's attention on his manifestation in their historical life. As interpreted by John, Jesus' response enables the community to come to terms with its earlier expectation of a final manifestation at the parousia. It is more important for the community to appreciate Jesus' manifestation in daily existence.

Today's reading includes the first part of Jesus' response (14:23-31). In vv. 23-26, Jesus recalls his earlier teaching (v. 25) that those who truly love him keep his words. Since Jesus' teaching comes from the Father (v. 24), those who live by it will enjoy the loving presence of both Jesus and his Father (v. 23). He then promises the Holy Spirit, who will instruct the disciples and bring to mind all he had taught.

In vv. 27-29, Jesus bestows his peace on his disciples as a farewell gift to preserve them from fear (v. 27) and help them accept his departure to the Father (v. 28). Once events have followed their course, the disciples will believe on the basis of Jesus' earlier teaching. Living in post-Easter fellowship, the community can transcend the disruption of the passion and see its life as the fulfillment of Jesus' life and message.

1. The church must always transcend its cultural roots to find new and varied expression among the peoples to whom it is sent (Acts 15:1-2, 22-29).

2. Christ's primary presence is in the church. We must not obscure Christ's image but make it more visible (Revelation 21:22).

3. Christ's peace (John 14:27) should help Christians confront life's challenges, disruptions and difficulties. His peace will keep us from seeking false, ultimately unsatisfying escapist solutions (John 14:23-29).

Ascension

The Ascension feast emphasizes the difference between life in the company of the historical Jesus and life in the post-Easter community. The New Testament does not see Jesus' absence as a problem. It is the result of his glorification at the Father's right hand, providing abundant blessings for the community and provoking the Christian mission in the Spirit's power. This is the portrait given by today's readings (Acts 1:1-11; Ephesians 1:17-23; Luke 24:46-53).

Acts 1:1-11

Acts 1:1-2, a brief recapitulation of the gospel, provides a smooth transition into the book. The focus here is the ascension, whose narrative closed Jesus' life in the gospel (Luke 24:50-53) and now serves to launch the church's life (Acts 1:9-11).

The ascension is a thematic element in Luke's theology of history. The church began in the community formed by Jesus and his disciples, but now it lived in the absence of the historical Jesus. Jesus' former mode of presence had ended. The church must recognize him in a new way and assume its Christian responsibility to continue his mission. In Luke's theology, the ascension serves to explain the church's life and mission.

Verse 3 summarizes the privileged 40 days during which the risen Lord instructed his disciples. The time evokes Israel's formative 40 years in the desert and Jesus' 40 days of testing. Jesus asked his disciples to await the Father's promised Spirit (vv. 4-5), cautioned them against preoccupation with the exact timing of the kingdom's restoration (vv. 6-7), and sketched the geographical outline of their mission (v. 8).

The account (vv. 9-11) is a symbolic statement of Jesus' going away. The end was not his death but his departure from history as a living person. The prospect of his return introduces a healthy tension into the church's life as it moves to definitive fulfillment.

Psalm 46:2-3, 6-7, 8-9

We praise God, king of all the earth (vv. 8-9) who reigns enthroned (v. 7). We celebrate him (vv. 2-3) because he chose us to receive Jacob's glory (v. 6). Liturgically, Jesus is our representative in his ascension-glorification, fulfilling our inheritance. Verse 6 describes Jesus the Lord, ascended to God's right hand, and serves as the assembly's response: "God mounts his throne to shouts of joy; a blare of trumpets for the Lord."

Ephesians 1:17-23

The church's life is here related to the heavenly Christ whom God has made ruler of all things and the church's head. In an opening prayer (vv. 17-19a), Paul asks the Father of glory to grant the Ephesians a clear knowledge of himself (v. 17). He wants God to enlighten them with the hope that is their heritage, so they can appreciate the power hope inspires among believers (vv. 18-19a). Here, hope does not mean the Christian virtue. It stands for hope's object, the foundation for a hopeful attitude and the reality that will one day fulfill it.

In vv. 19b-21, the power born of hope is compared to the strength God displayed in raising Jesus to exalted life. The comparison is appropriate because hope's object is a share in Christ's risen life. The divine power is reflected in believers as the pledge of their future inheritance. Christ has

already received the fullness of hope's promise. As Christ's body, the
church is assured of the hope realized in its head.

Luke 24:46-53

The ending of Luke's gospel includes a manifestation of the risen Lord
to a troubled community of disciples and closes with that community's
joyful response to Jesus' ascension. The transformation in the community's attitude was effected first by Jesus' assurance that Christian table
fellowship provides an experience of the same Jesus who had suffered and
died for them (24:36-44). Although Jesus is now the risen Lord and his
mode of presence to the community is altogether different, there is a
fundamental continuity between their past and present experience of him.

Another element in the change of the community's attitude involves
Jesus' opening their minds to understand recent events (v. 45). The meaning of Jesus' passion-resurrection is summarized in light of the scriptures
(v. 46). On the secure basis of this biblical reflection, the Christians are
freed for the mission Jesus describes (vv. 47-48). Jesus' followers could not
place recent events in the continuum of biblical history; with their minds
opened, they could now face the future. They had to prepare for the gospel
mission which they were to launch from Jerusalem after being endowed
with divine power (v. 49). As the site of the gospel's fulfillment in Jesus'
resurrection, Jerusalem would also be the place of its initial proclamation.

The Christian community could now cope with Jesus' departure (vv.
50-53). A sad and terrifying event, Jesus' death and the community's
experience of loss, had been transformed into Jesus' entry into new life and
an experience of gain, a joyful event to be celebrated in praise of God.

> *1. Like the early Christians, we too confront Jesus' depar-
> ture, as particular historical forms of religion disappear or
> evolve. Christian readiness asks us to look to the future (Acts
> 1:1-11).*
>
> *2. With the author, we pray for an experiential understand-
> ing of the extraordinary grace of Christian existence (Ephesians
> 1:17-23).*
>
> *3. By situating our lives in the history of God's presence to
> his people, we can celebrate our faith freely and joyfully (Luke
> 24:46-53).*

Seventh Sunday of Easter

*Throughout history, we are sustained by Jesus' prayer as we
try to maintain unity in the love he first manifested to us (John
17:20-26). That love is forgiving because those forgiven must
also forgive. It will introduce us into the vision of Christ (Acts
7:55-60). With Revelation 22:12-14, 16-17, 20 we eagerly look
forward to its consummation in Christ's coming.*

Acts 7:55-60

Luke's history of Christian origins at Jerusalem (3:1-8:3) climaxes in the
story of Stephen's martyrdom (6:8-8:3), an account partially modeled on
the last moments of Jesus' life. Just as Jesus' passion marked the end of a
period of history and provided a transition to the church's life, Stephen's
passion terminated the first phase in the church's life and provided the
transition to the community's mission away from Jerusalem. Henceforth,
Luke's interest in Jerusalem would be limited to the mother community's
relationship to the new communities.

The comparison between Stephen and Jesus is particularly striking in
their last words. Jesus' prayer, "Father, forgive them; they do not know
what they are doing" (Luke 23:34), is echoed by Stephen's "Lord, do not
hold this sin against them" (7:60). Jesus' final cry, "Father, into your hands
I commend my spirit" (Luke 23:46) reverberates in Stephen's "Lord Jesus,
receive my spirit" (7:59).

The differences between the last words are also significant. It may no
longer have been possible to say the persecutors did not know what they
were doing (cf. 7:53). Further, while Jesus had prayed "Father," Stephen's
prayer was addressed to the Lord Jesus. Stephen's invocation must be
understood in light of his vision of Jesus as the Son of Man standing at
God's right hand (7:55-56). As the fulfillment of Jesus' announcement in
Mark 14:62, the vision marks a new moment in God's historical intervention. Jesus is now revealed as God's judge and Stephen addresses his prayer
accordingly.

In effect, the text transforms the Sanhedrin's judgment on Stephen into a
divine judgment on Jerusalem. Stephen's condemnation and martyrdom
were viewed positively as the divinely intended beginning of the church's
rapid spread away from Jerusalem.

Psalm 97:1-2, 6-7, 9

A royal psalm sings of God's dominion and summons us to worship our divine king (v. 1). It describes his manifestation in creation (v. 2a) and history (v. 2b). The entire universe proclaims his justice and glory (vv. 6-7). We confess his sovereignty because he exceeds every other divinity (v. 9). The community responds: "The Lord is king, the most high over all the earth."

Revelation 22:12-14, 16-17, 20

This last in a series of readings from the book of Revelation draws on verses included in the book's epilogue (22:6-21).

Great emphasis is placed on the imminence of Christ's return (vv. 7, 12, 20). In v. 7 Christ's coming had been presented as a blessing for those who heed Revelation's prophetic message. In v. 12 the same statement is spelled out more concretely in terms of reward for good conduct. Insistence on retribution at the end of time is characteristic of apocalyptic literature. The attitude springs largely from the fact that present events give little or no evidence of retributive justice.

In v. 20, the author and the community he represents look forward to Christ's coming with joy. They even make it the object of their prayer. In this they are united with the prayer of the Spirit and the bride (v. 17), that is, the prophets and the saints (16:6; 18:24). The words "Come, Lord Jesus!" were very likely from the early Christian liturgy. We find them in similar form in 1 Corinthians 16:22. They are a plea for Christ's manifestation in glory at the parousia.

By focusing our attention on Christ's ultimate return in glory, the liturgy helps us appreciate his manifestation day by day in the church's life. As we pray "Come, Lord Jesus!", we assume our Christian responsibility for bringing about Christ's return and for developing the Christian community into an ever sharper image of Christ.

John 17:20-26

Jesus' farewell discourse concludes with the most extensive, comprehensive prayer attributed to him in the New Testament. Addressed by the Son to his Father (17:1, 5, 11, 21, 24, 25), the prayer expresses what had already been promised in scripture (v. 12). Like the scriptures, Jesus' prayer would surely be fulfilled. During Jesus' passion and in future persecutions and difficulties, the prayer would be recalled as an abiding source of security. Whatever suffering life might bring, the Christians had the assurance of Jesus' prayer on their behalf.

Today's reading is the concluding section of the prayer and of the farewell discourse. Jesus prays not only for the disciples who had joined him for this final meal but for all future generations of followers. The passage explicitly broadens Jesus' message to include the church's life. In fact, the entire farewell discourse had the future church in view. In 17:20-26, however, many themes already developed are presented anew in relation to Christian unity. Already a long-standing problem, the unity of the church in the love of Jesus and his Father was a major challenge confronted by John's gospel. It still speaks to all who take the fragmentation of our Christianity seriously.

> 1. *New Testament writers frequently saw the pattern of Christ's death-resurrection reflected in later events. This enabled them to draw hope out of tragedy (Acts 7:55-60).*
>
> 2. *Although events may be troublesome, Christians live with the deeper security that Christ's prayer on their behalf will be fulfilled (John 17:20-26).*
>
> 3. *Our model for church unity is the relationship between Christ and his Father (John 17:20-26).*

Pentecost

Three readings about the gift of the Spirit to the Christian community highlight Pentecost's extraordinary meaning. In the first and third lessons, the Spirit's energizing power accompanied the birth of Christianity. That power issued from God (Acts 2:1-11) and was communicated by Christ the glorified Lord (John 20:19-23). In the second reading, the Spirit continues his presence in the church through the gift of creative ministries for the common good (1 Corinthians 12:3-7, 12-13).

Acts 2:1-11

Pentecost was one of the three major festivals in the ancient Israelite calendar. Passover initiated the grain harvest; and Pentecost, celebrated seven weeks (50 days) later, marked harvest's end. Passover acquired historical significance at a very early date. Pentecost persisted as an agricultural festival throughout the Old Testament period.

The historicizing of Pentecost came in the first and second centuries

A.D. Rabbinical Judaism associated Pentecost with the granting of the law to Moses. The festival marked Israel's birth at the foot of Mount Sinai. For the early Christians, Pentecost celebrated the birth of the universal church as the new Israel.

Luke's account of the first Christian Pentecost is one of the New Testament's most profound reflections on the church's origins and nature. He emphasized two points in his narrative: the church's newness, and its universality.

The church's birth is a new moment in biblical history. The sound *like* a wind powerfully symbolizes this newness. The comparison recalls the wind that hovered over the waters at the first creation (Genesis 1:2) and the wind that was God's breath in man's creation as a living being (Genesis 2:7). In Acts 2:2, the wind is God's Spirit, effecting a new creation and filling the church with God's creative life force. The tongues *like* fire (2:3) represent God's purifying, sanctifying presence, consecrating the church as prophetic speaker of God's word.

The unit strongly affirms the church's universality by emphasizing the many nations represented in the apostles' audience. In spite of cultural and linguistic differences, everyone understands the apostles' message about God's marvelous deeds (2:5-11). The church's birth institutes a new order of human communication. It reverses the disarray of primeval Babel (Genesis 11:1-9) where human beings had ceased to understand each other.

Psalm 103:1ab, 24ac, 29bc-30, 31, 34

Psalm 103 is a hymn in praise of God's creative wisdom and power. His greatness appears as creative generosity (vv. 1ab, 24ac). By sending his breath or spirit, God creates and renews life; when he withdraws it, everything returns to dust (vv. 29bc-30). The last strophe voices our hope in God's enduring glory, manifested in creation (vv. 31, 34). The community's prayerful response ("Lord, send out your Spirit, and renew the face of the earth") is inspired by v. 30a. Our liturgical use of the verse comes in light of the New Testament's experience of God's personal, creative Holy Spirit.

1 Corinthians 12:3-7, 12-13

In response to problems in Corinth, Paul instructed the Christian community at length about spiritual gifts (1 Corinthians 12-14). Various interpretations of the gifts' importance and their manifestation in the assembly had caused conflict. In today's reading, Paul affirms the gifts' fundamental importance and their complementarity.

No one can proclaim faith in Jesus as Lord without the Holy Spirit, and no person will curse Jesus if he truly speaks in the Spirit. The quality of faith is the criterion for discerning the Spirit's presence (v. 3).

Paul wants to maintain unity in the manifestation of the gifts, so he emphasizes how persons with different gifts complement each other. He invokes the metaphor of the body and its many members (12:12-31). This analogy was already developed in ancient philosophical writing; but, very likely, the early Christian understanding of the eucharistic assembly as a sharing in Christ's body suggested its use to Paul.

Those who share in the Lord's supper become one body (1 Corinthians 11:23-29). The reference to Christ in 12:12 includes both Christ's person and the community members in whom he is present. Whatever their origins, all baptized Christians formed one body in Christ (12:13a). By drinking the one cup, everyone shared in the same Spirit (12:13b).

John 20:19-23

Luke associated the church's birth in the Spirit with the Jewish feast of Pentecost. John tied it to Jesus' resurrection on Easter Sunday (20:19). Whatever the importance of this variance between the two evangelists, another difference is far more significant. In Luke, the Spirit is the Father's gift (Acts 2:2-4) in fulfillment of the Father's promise (Luke 24:49, Acts 1:4). In John 20:19-23, Jesus gives the Spirit directly during an appearance to the assembled disciples. The Johannine author relates the church's life in the Spirit to the person of the risen Lord.

Verse 19a emphasizes the spiritual quality of the risen Lord, not subject to spatio-temporal limitations. At the same time, the risen Lord is the same person whose historical life had ended with death on a cross (v. 20). Both vv. 19b and 21a include Jesus' characteristic greeting, "Peace be with you" (see p. 67). Although Jesus is historically absent and the disciples have known sadness (16:22), they continue to find peace in his risen presence. Peace has been his farewell gift to them (14:27, 16:33). Renewed in Christ's peace, the disciples receive the mission Jesus had received from the Father (21:21b, 17:18).

The Spirit given the disciples is the risen Lord's breath. This striking evocation of Genesis 2:7 is a powerful Christological statement. The first man had become a living being when God breathed life into him; now the disciples receive new life when the risen Lord breathes his Spirit-filled life into them. Quickened by the Lord's Spirit, the disciples share his power of reconciliation (20:33), to be exercised with the peace that had characterized Jesus' attitude toward sinners.

   1. Pentecost summarizes the origins of the post-Easter community as the church's birth (Acts 2:1-11).

   2. Fidelity to origins requires the church to be a community in which there are no barriers to communication and all grow in the one Spirit that gave them life (Acts 2:5-11).

   3. In the work of reconciliation, all Christians must manifest the Spirit of peace with which Christ brings us to life (John 20:19-23).

Ordinary Time

Second Sunday of the Year

Christians are called to reflect on the fundamental signs of God's creative presence in their lives. For the Johannine community, the Cana event was such a sign (John 2:1-12). The wedding feast expressed their transformation into a new people. We project it liturgically against Isaiah 62:1-5, where a promised name change indicates new, God-given identity. The second reading articulates the complementarity and unity of those who share this new identity (1 Corinthians 12:4-11).

Isaiah 62:1-5

A song of Trito-Isaiah provides a broad biblical setting for the Cana wedding feast. In Isaiah 62:1-5, Jerusalem becomes the Lord's spouse. By implication, Cana is a celebration of Yahweh's nuptials with his people. The divine wedding is a frequent theme, especially in prophetic literature, to show the meaning of Israel's covenant relationship with God.

In v. 1 the Lord refers to Jerusalem in the third person. He states his firm intention to stand by her until she is firmly established. Historically, the poem reflects the difficult days immediately after Israel's return from the exile (587-538 B.C.) at the end of the 6th century.

The body (vv. 2-5) alludes to Jerusalem's recognition by the nations at whose hands she had suffered (v. 2a). She is to have a new God-given name (v. 2b) to designate her new and glorious relationship with God (v. 3). Verses 3-5 sing of the effects of God's action on Jerusalem's behalf. Old names, like "Forsaken" and "Desolate," will no longer apply. Jerusalem will be called "My delight" and "Espoused" because this will be her true condition (v. 4a). The remainder of the hymn identifies the source of Jerusalem's new names as God's loving action on her behalf (vv. 4b-5).

Psalm 96:1-2, 2-3, 7-8, 9-10

God's saving act (Isaiah 62:1-5) is celebrated with a hymn extolling his royal dominion and summoning the universe to join in worshipful song. Since God's salvation is newly manifested (v. 2b), it calls for a new song to declare his glorious works before all peoples (vv. 1-3). The public acknowledgement of God's glorious might (vv. 7-8) leads to worship and the ceremonial proclamation of his kingship (vv. 9-10). After each strophe, the assembly responds: "Proclaim his marvelous deeds to all the nations."

1 Corinthians 12:4-11

In early Christianity, as here in 1 Corinthians 12:4-11, the term *charism* had a broader meaning than its usage in our day. In vv. 4-6, gifts or charisms, ministries and works all refer to the same Christian realities. In relation to the Spirit, the Father's gift sent by Christ, they are best designated as gifts (v. 4). In relation to the Son, the Lord whose life purpose was essentially to minister, the term ministries is most appropriate (v. 5). Finally, in relation to the Father, whose creative work never ceases, the gifts or ministries may also be called works (v. 6).

There is a wide diversity among the gifts and their distribution in the community. This was a source of conflict and division among the Corinthians, especially when they gathered for their assemblies. As elsewhere in 1 Corinthians, Paul argues strongly for unity. Diversity in the manifestation of gifts must not obscure the one Spirit who grants them (vv. 4, 11) or impede the common good for which they are granted (v. 7).

John 2:1-12

The Johannine narrative of the wedding feast at Cana is not a simple miracle story. Multiple symbolic significance can be attributed to nearly every element in the account. Indeed the entire event is a sign (v. 11). Even the seventh day on which the sign was effected is significant. The sign at Cana is the first of Jesus' signs in the sense that it is the primary or principle one, at the climax of the new creation. Writing on different levels, John presents the same seventh day as the third (2:1) to relate the Cana event to the resurrection and glorification of Jesus.

The principal sign of the new creation, which includes all others, is the transformation of the old covenant, symbolized by water in jars for Jewish purification (vv. 6-7), into the new covenant with its superior wine (vv. 8-10). The change was effected when Jesus' hour had come (17:1), that is, at the moment of his glorification when he was raised up and water and blood flowed from his side (19:34). In light of John's general sacramental interest, the event must also be seen as symbolic of the eucharist, in which the new covenant is celebrated as the risen Lord's wedding feast.

The dialogue between Jesus and the woman (vv. 3-4), in which Jesus disavows the woman's request, and the subsequent narrative in which Jesus fulfills that request reflect the event's two levels, the sign and the signified. As a historical event in the life of Jesus (sign), his hour had not yet come; as a later theological expression of the meaning of Jesus' life and its eucharistic implications (signified), the hour had arrived. The term "woman" recalls Eve, the mother of the new creation.

> *1. Each member or group of members in the Christian community must direct its charisms or ministries to the unity of the entire community (1 Corinthians 12:7).*
>
> *2. The effect of Jesus' life, death and glorification was the transformation of the old covenant into the new (John 2:1-12).*
>
> *3. Historical events in Jesus' life are signs of the church's life. They communicate on both these levels (John 2:1-12).*

Third Sunday of the Year

Our work in the church builds on New Testament foundations, just as Luke-Acts (Luke 1:1-4) built on Jesus' word and work. That work is summarized in Jesus' inaugural self-presentation in the Nazareth synagogue (Luke 4:14-21). As the manifestation of a new divine dispensation, it fulfills God's gift of the Torah as presented in Nehemiah 8:2-4, 5-6, 8-10. 1 Corinthians 12:12-30 shows how the new law is deployed in the community of Christ's body.

Nehemiah 8:2-4, 5-6, 8-10

The first reading is from the Chronicler's account of Ezra's promulgation of the law. The written law is Israel's literary record of the Torah, henceforth universally accepted in Israel as God's normative word. It now forms the first and most fundamental part of trhe Hebrew Bible, the five books from Genesis to Deuteronomy, the Pentateuch. The term law should not be understood as legislation in a modern sense, but as Judaism's way of life, given in the life-narratives of the great ancestors Abraham, Isaac, Jacob, Joseph and Moses.

The law was read first to the assembly of Israel who listened attentively (vv. 2-3). In the presence of Israel's leaders and the entire gathering, Ezra the scribe then raised the law aloft that all might see it (vv. 4-5). He blessed God, and the people manifested their "Amen" by prostrating in worship (v. 6). Reading on, Ezra interpreted the law (v. 8) and proclaimed the day of its promulgation as a day of celebration in Israel (vv. 9-10).

The liturgy presents this passage as the antecedent for the new reading, interpretation and fulfillment of the law undertaken by Jesus (cf. today's gospel).

Psalm 19:8, 9, 10, 15

In the Pentateuch's priestly tradition, the giving of the law provides the pattern for the story of creation. Similarly, Psalm 19 presents God both as creator and as giver of the law. We praise the law and its refreshing wisdom (v. 8) and extoll its justice and clarity, causes for rejoicing and enlightenment (v. 9). We focus on its enduring quality (v. 10), pray for divine favor and proclaim God as our firm redemption (v. 15). Our response is from the New Testament, "Your words, Lord, are spirit and life" (John 6:64).

1 Corinthians 12:12-30

Continuing the discussion of unity in diversity introduced last Sunday (see p. 90), the liturgy takes up Paul's famous analogy of the body of Christ. Although later centuries would develop Paul's elaborate metaphor in terms of a mystical body, this later notion is not very helpful for understanding 1 Corinthians. Since the union of many members in Christ is sacramentally effected (v. 13) and is itself a visible sign of the risen Christ (v. 12), the term "sacramental body" would be far more appropriate.

To demonstrate the importance of diverse roles in the community, Paul develops at great length the analogy of the human body with its many fuctional parts and organs. Even the least is indispensable (vv. 14-26). In vv. 27-30, he applies the analogy to the Corinthian community whose members are richly but diversely endowed with God's gifts.

Luke 1:1-4; 4:14-21

This reading joins Luke's preface (1:1-4) and the beginning of Jesus' inaugural self-presentation in the synagogue of Nazareth (4:14-21).

The Lukan preface has long been recognized as a high point in New Testament literary expression. Assuming the style of a Hellenistic historian, Luke reviews the history of the gospel's transmission. He gives his reason for writing, the manner in which he went about his task and the goal he hopes to achieve. The person addressed, Theophilus, meaning "beloved by God," could well represent all of Luke's intended readers. The passage demonstrates Christianity's continuing need to reinterpret the gospel in light of new historical situations.

The Nazareth episode (4:14-30) illustrates Luke's extraordinary sensitivity to language's evocative power and his keen sense of the dramatic. Following an introductory summary of Jesus' work in Galilee (4:14-15), the first part of the text proceeds in three movements. Today's reading interrupts this development at v. 21.

Jesus quotes from Isaiah 61:1-2. The passage evokes Jesus' public ministry as a direct fulfillment of scripture and indirectly as God's response to Israel's messianic expectations (4:18-19). The Isaiah citation is framed in a chiseled statement of Jesus' movements before and after the reading (4:16-17, 20). Insignificant details draw attention to Jesus and to the importance of his message. Isaiah 61:1-2 is Jesus' gospel.

Jesus indicates that the passage read is actually fulfilled in the very hearing of the Nazareth synagogue (4:21). In Isaiah 61:1-2, the gospel remained in promise. In the personal communication of Jesus, it springs to life and is now a reality.

1. Isaiah 61:1-2 is a summary of Jesus' life for Christians of every historical period. Who then are the poor, the blind and the captives of today (Luke 4:14-21)?

2. What consequences may we draw for daily life from the fact that we are one in Christ's body (1 Corinthians 12:12-30)?

3. How does the Old Testament apply to Christians today (Nehemiah 8:2-4, 5-6, 8-10; Luke 4:14-21)?

Fourth Sunday of the Year

Christ's work goes beyond our expectations: it is addressed to

*all peoples. As with the Jews of Nazareth, that universality
often threatens us. Their effort to destroy Jesus is a warning
(Luke 4:21-30). Like Jesus and Jeremiah before him, we must
take up this universal mission and fearlessly confront opposition (Jeremiah 1:4-5, 17-19). As men and women who genuinely
love (1 Corinthians 12:31-13:13) we shall pass safely through
opposition (Luke 4:30).*

Jeremiah 1:4-5, 17-19

Jeremiah's vocation narrative includes a dialogue between the Lord and
Jeremiah (1:4-10, 17-19) and two visions (1:11-16). Today's reading consists
of the dialogue's first and last sections. They focus on the prophet and on
God's action equipping him for his prophetic role. The text's emphasis on
a mission to the nations or gentiles and Israel's anticipated opposition
provides a precedent for Jesus' prophetic mission in the gospel.

In Jeremiah 1:4-5, the Lord's word addresses Jeremiah on his preparation for prophethood. The prophet's divine mission antedates his conception and birth. It flows from God's eternal providence and has been
inscribed by the creator in his very being. Response to God's call cannot be
a light matter. The prophetic function is intimately bound with the
meaning of Jeremiah's existence.

Jeremiah's mission to the gentiles must be seen against the background
of Israel's universal mission. God's people had been called from among the
nations to be an instrument of his word and work on their behalf. This
aspect of Israel's vocation was muted and implicit during the early years. It
came to the fore after maturation when Israel felt strong in its selfhood,
particularly when she confronted the gentiles' military threat as in Jeremiah's time. The actualization of Israel's universal mission was not effected
without resistance from within. God, however, strengthened the prophet.
His designs would surely prevail (vv. 17-19).

Psalm 71:1-2, 3-4, 5-6, 15-17

With the psalmist we lament our situation and plead for God's help.
God is our fortress, a safe refuge; he is our rock, sturdy, steadfast and
worthy of complete trust (vv. 1-4). Hope and trust are the themes of vv. 5-6.
In vv. 15-17, we pledge to praise God in the future as we have in the past.
This inspires the assembly's response, "I will sing of your salvation."

1 Corinthians 12:31-13:13

Having discussed the Spirit's gifts, their purpose (1 Corinthians 12:4-11), and their complementarity (vv. 12-30), Paul now turns to their essential hierarchy (12:31-13:13). He treats especially the greatest gift of all, the gift of love which gives meaning to the others.

The gift of love is not to be confused with an exclusively human love channeled into altruistic generosity (v. 3). The love of which Paul speaks is divine love, God's love "sacramentally" expressed in the love of Christians. Rather than our love for God, it is God's love for us, a love manifested in our loving. Without this love, every other seeming gift is an empty, meaningless sham (13:1-3).

The fine rhetoric of 13:1-3 now becomes almost poetic as Paul sings the concrete attributes and social expressions of genuine love (vv. 4-7). To appreciate this lyrical development, the reader should recall the disturbances at Corinth which occasioned Paul's concern and the present passage. In vv. 8-13, Paul situates love in terms of the Christian's personal history, which tends toward ever greater perfection until the day when only faith, hope and love remain, with love as the greatest.

Luke 4:21-30

In this reading, the liturgy resumes the account of Jesus' Nazareth experience (4:14-30). Repeating 4:21, with which last week's gospel ended, the text includes the end of the unit's first section (4:22) and the narrative's entire second, final part (4:23-30).

In 4:22, Luke dwells on the audience's amazement. He interprets its reaction in the narrative's third direct quotation: "Is not this Joseph's son?" Jesus' words and the manner in which he applied them to himself and indirectly to the recipients of the gospel, raise the question of Jesus' true identity among those who had seen him grow up (v. 16). The question rings in the ears of Jesus' first hearers and in the lives of all who even now have the gospel preached to them.

The second part of the Nazareth synagogue episode outlines Jesus' address to his auditors and their response. It contrasts quite sharply with the first. Part one had ended on a positive note, albeit interrogatory; part two presents the negative, indeed violent, reaction of the people of Jesus' home town (vv. 28-30). This reaction had been provoked by Jesus' challenge. He announced that, as in the days of Elijah and Elisha, the gospel would be proclaimed to the gentiles, not to the Jews (vv. 23-27). In spite of efforts to destroy him, Jesus proceeds straight through their midst (v. 30b).

From the audience's point of view the event ends on a negative note, but the passage as a whole concludes on the upbeat.

> *1. What is the meaning of Christian "love of God" (1 Corinthians 13:1-3)?*
>
> *2. How does love relate to other aspects of Christian behavior (1 Corinthians 13:4-7)?*
>
> *3. The question of Jesus' identity, in New Teatament times as today, is a personal question that requires a personal answer (Luke 4:22).*

Fifth Sunday of the Year

The call to discipleship is grounded in an experience of God's wonderful signs on our behalf. It presupposes a faith response to Christ the Lord. Simon Peter is our model (Luke 5:1-11). His call is part of a long history of divine calls for special missions. Among these, the liturgy has selected Isaiah's for our reflection (Isaiah 6:1-2, 3-8). For Christians, however, the call is now based on an experience of the risen Lord (1 Corinthians 15:1-11).

Isaiah 6:1-2, 3-8

This reading includes the first part (6:1-8) of the dialogue in which Isaiah responds to his prophetic vocation (6:1-13). As in today's second and third texts, the human response to divine call follows a tremendous experience of God's presence.

In a description reminiscent of the great theophany at Sinai (Exodus 19:16-19), after which the people of Israel were called to be God's people (24:1-11), God's glory threatens to overwhelm Isaiah (6:1-4). Isaiah's religious experience is projected against Israel's fundamental experience. Although the event is in the temple at a particular point in time (6:1), it should be viewed as a summary statement of Isaiah's continuing experience of God, which took a new turn in the year king Uzziah died. The cry of the seraphim, "Holy, holy, holy," is now used in the liturgy.

Isaiah's response to the divine manifestation is a dialogue (vv. 5-8). Protesting his lack of holiness, Isaiah considers himself unworthy of God's presence and consequently doomed by God's overpowering holiness (v. 5). God, however, does not leave Isaiah at a distance, but purifies him with his own holiness, symbolically expressed by the application of a burning ember to the prophet's lips (vv. 6-7). Thereupon, Isaiah can interpret God's presence as an invitation to assume a prophetic role in Israel, to express in his life and word the vocation of God's covenanted people. Purified by God's presence, Isaiah exclaims: "Here I am, send me!" (v. 8).

Psalm 138: 1-2, 2-3, 4-5, 7-8

Like Isaiah at the moment of his call, the psalmist stands in the temple court with this prayer of thanksgiving for life and liberation. Gratitude is inseparable from worship (vv. 1-2); both follow upon God's kind response to prayer (vv. 2-3). The psalmist's horizon extends to all of earth's kings. What God has done will move them to glorify the Lord (vv. 4-5) as God continues the work of salvation he has begun (vv. 7-8). The assembly greets each strophe with: "In the sight of the angels I will sing your praises, Lord."

1 Corinthians 15:1-11

The first part of 1 Corinthians 15 focuses on Christ's resurrection and the manifestation of the risen Lord to his followers. It introduces Paul's main statement on the resurrection of Christians (15:12-58). The introduction is so rich and extraordinary that the liturgy can utilize it in isolation.

Paul begins by pointing out that the gospel he had preached at Corinth (about 50 A.D.) was the traditional gospel he himself had received. He thus refers to the days of his Christian development at Antioch in the early and mid-'40s. He stresses the fact that the Corinthians accepted the gospel and persisted in their belief (vv. 1-3a, 11).

In 15:3b-5, Paul quotes one of the oldest Christian creeds. As a formulation of faith, this creed is simple but compact, including the basic points of belief along with their significance and the manner in which the Christians had arrived at their formulation. After a number of additional credal formulas (vv. 6-7), Paul includes himself as one favored by an appearance of Christ (vv. 8-10). He draws the line of the historical creed to his own time, indicating that his experience of Christ is a point of departure for both his faith and his apostolic work. He invites us to do the same.

Luke 5:1-11

Luke's narrative of the call of the first disciples blends many elements of gospel tradition into an extremely rich account. To appreciate the author's theological and literary accomplishment, read Mark 4:1-2, 1:16-20 and John 21:1-18, where the various elements appear in distinct contexts.

Luke provides a setting by the Lake of Gennesaret. A crowd has come to hear God's word and Jesus responds with his teaching. He steps into a boat, which pulls out a short distance from the shore at his request. The boat belongs to Simon, a principal figure in the narrative (vv. 1-3).

Having manifested himself in speaking God's word, Jesus reveals himself in an action even more revelatory of God's presence. Simon is ordered to set out into the deep and lower his nets. Recalling their earlier lack of success, Simon nevertheless acts on Jesus' word. The extraordinary catch leads to the call of Simon and his partners James and John (vv. 4-7).

Aware of the extraordinary divine character of Jesus' work and deed, Simon Peter acknowledges his sinfulness. Jesus calms his fears and indicates Simon's future mission. With that, Simon and his companions become Jesus' followers (vv. 8-11).

> *1. The call to divine service is accompanied by God's purifying presence enabling us to assume our vocation with courage (Isaiah 6:1-8).*
>
> *2. Our faith and mission are founded in an experience of the risen Lord (1 Corinthians 15:1-11).*
>
> *3. The Christian impetus for following Christ (Luke 5:8-11) is a response to his manifestation to us in word and deed (Luke 5:1-3, 4-7).*

Sixth Sunday of the Year

Jesus' beatitudes and woes (Luke 6:17, 20-26) sensitize us to Christian values and move us to a decision. This mode of teaching is based on a long tradition of sapiential communication, whose elements are included in Jeremiah 17:5-8. In 1 Corinthians 15:12, 16-20, we reflect on our commitment in light of the resurrection of those who have joined Christ in his way.

Jeremiah 17:5-8

The first reading is from a collection of three sapiential sayings in the book of Jeremiah (17:5-8, 9-10, 11). The unit, out of context, appears intrusive. Be that as it may, Jeremiah 17:5-8 is a good example of the traditional style and method of wisdom teaching. The passage is very likely the inspiration for Psalm 1, which applies Jeremiah's saying on trust in the Lord (vv. 7-8) to joyful meditation on the law (Psalm 1:2-3).

Jeremiah pronounces the Lord's curse on the person who trusts in human beings (vv. 5-6) and his blessing on those who trust in the Lord (vv. 7-8). Contrasting the two, he draws a comparison with vegetable life. The former is a barren bush wasting in a desert place like the area around the Dead Sea. The latter is a tree flourishing beside a hospitable stream even during the year's long dry season. The simile's strength lies in its evocative imagery as a biblical setting for the gospel reading. Today's liturgy calls upon this ancient beatitude and malediction as background for the gospel.

Psalm 1:1-2, 3, 4, 6

Psalm 1, an introduction to the psalter, indicates that, from the compilers' point of view, Israel's worship is a source of wisdom. This wisdom psalm begins with a beatitude about a person's relationship to the law (vv. 1-2). The just person who delights in the law is ever close to the source of life and refreshment (v. 3); by contrast, the wicked dries up and vanishes with the wind (vv. 4, 6). The response is from Psalm 39:5, "Happy are they who hope in the Lord."

1 Corinthians 15:12, 16-20

The second reading picks up 1 Corinthians 15 where last Sunday's liturgy left off, drawing out the implications of Christ's resurrection for belief in the resurrection of all Christians (vv. 12, 16-19). Omitted are Paul's reflections on the emptiness of his preaching in the absence of this faith (vv. 13-15).

The reading concludes with the affirmation that Christ's resurrection is not an isolated phenomenon but the first of many (v. 20). This statement in context introduces vv. 20-28, prepared by Paul's reference to those who died (fell asleep) in Christ (v. 18). They are in Christ, and Christ is no longer dead but risen. They must consequently rise with him.

Paul's basic point is that if the Corinthians hold there is no resurrection from the dead, they must be consistent and deny Christ's resurrection. As they themselves admit, this would eliminate the cornerstone of their faith (vv. 12, 16). By rejecting the one resurrection while holding the other, they are inconsistent.

Paul reinforces the point by a hypothetical situation in which Christ would not have been raised: the Corinthians' faith would be worthless; they would still be in their sins; the dead would be just dead and hope would be limited to this life. Implied are the role of Christ's resurrection in the work of redemption and the emptiness of life without the hope of afterlife.

Luke 6:17, 20-26

In Luke 6:17-49, Matthew's more ample sermon on the mount (5-7) is a sermon on the plain. Today's reading includes the introductory verse along with the beatitudes and the woes. Omitted is the summary of prior activity that demonstrates Jesus' power and established the context for his authoritative pronouncements.

The first part of Jesus' address to the crowd of Jews and gentiles (v. 17) is divided into two carefully balanced sermons. Three beatitudes (vv. 20-21) correspond to three maledictions (vv. 24-25). Each section is amplified by an additional beatitude (vv. 22-23a) and woe (v. 26a) that depart from the established structure. At least the extra beatitude represents a later but pre-Lukan development of tradition (cf. Matthew 5:11-12). Each section concludes with the historical observation that this is how the fathers treated the prophets (v. 23b; cf. Matthew 5:12b) and the false prophets (v. 26b). Parallelism is closely maintained throughout the unit.

A beatitude (cf. Psalm 1:1) is a joyful congratulation. In Matthew the object is spiritualized (e.g. "poor in spirit"); Luke addressed the concrete social condition of Jesus' hearers. Interpreters are struck by the beatitudes' paradoxical nature. Whatever their original meaning, early tradition and Luke saw them as a statement that the poor, the hungry and the sorrowful have good grounds to rejoice in spite of their situation. They can expect a great reward in heaven (v. 23). The opposite is true for the rich, the full and the merry. In both cases, a precedent could be adduced from the life of the prophets and the manner in which they were treated. The strength of the expressions is their hyperbolic ability to awaken the hearer to the deepest and most genuine values.

> *1. The contrast between the person who trusts in human beings and the person who trusts in the Lord provokes reflection on a secular value system that excludes God from human life (Jeremiah 17:5-8).*

> *2. Faith in Christ's resurrection, intimately linked to that of Christians, is the springboard of Christian hope (1 Corinthians 15:12, 16-20).*

3. *Christian life is paradoxical. Who is truly rich and who is really poor (Luke 6:20-26)?*

Seventh Sunday of the Year

Christians give human expression to God's selfless love. Jesus spells out the ramifications of this active relationship to God and people (Luke 6:27-38). Like David, Christians refuse to distinguish between friend and foe (1 Samuel 26:2, 7-9, 12-13, 22-23). Non-discriminating love is the only fitting attitude for those destined one day to leave their earthly body behind and to take up a Spirit-filled body (1 Corinthians 15:45-49).

1 Samuel 26:2, 7-9, 12-13, 22-23

In its liturgical form, the reading includes four short segments of an account in which David spares the life of Saul (1 Samuel 26:1-25). Although essential elements have been retained, the story has lost most of its sense of movement and dramatic intensity. We can no longer account for the protagonists' behavior.

Some lectionaries retain "but David answered" in v. 22, when Saul's prior statement (v. 21) has been dropped. In effect, we are presented with a new story possessing few of the qualities found in the original biblical account. Such drastic, badly executed abbreviations do little to promote appreciation of the biblical word. The preacher would be wise to consult a Bible for the original.

The passage appears to have been selected as a prototype of Christian love which refuses to distinguish between friend and enemy (cf. gospel reading). In the theological context of 1 Samuel, however, David spares Saul's life because of his sacred character as God's anointed (vv. 9, 11, 16, 23).

Psalm 103:1-2, 3-4, 8, 10, 12-13

An individual has been struck down by disease and brought close to death (the Pit). His recovery leads to thankful prayer (vv. 1-5). God heals and forgives (vv. 3-4), so we bless his name (vv. 1-2). Unlike us, he is merciful and does not deal with us according to our sins (vv. 8, 10). Boundless in mercy, he is a father to us his children (vv. 12-13).

1 Corinthians 15:45-49

For the third consecutive Sunday, the second reading is from 1 Corinthians 15, Paul's most extensive discussion of the resurrection of Christ and his followers. Paul distinguished between the natural body, in which humans live this historical life and die, and the spiritual body, in which they rise. Now he sets out his understanding of those bodies (vv. 45-49). The development supports his prior affirmation that there is indeed a spiritual body (15:44b).

Paul contrasts Christ with Adam. Reference is made to God's breathing life into the clay from which he had formed the man, thereby making him a living being (Genesis 2:7). He turns to Christ, the last Adam, who by his resurrection had become spirit. Adam had *received* life in the moment of his creation. Christ's resurrection made him live-*giving* (v. 45). This, Paul insists, is the order of things, first the natural then the spiritual (v. 46). The point is a response to those who might believe that already they are risen with Christ. Christ's risen state is from heaven, unlike Adam's life which is from earth. Only when our earthly life is ended do we come to resemble Christ in his heavenly spiritual body (vv. 48-49).

The passage reflects Paul's struggle to interpret the risen life for Greeks. Jews grasped it intuitively, but Greeks showed more concern for analytical dissection of human nature. Paul's concept of resurrection transcends the "natural" immortality of the soul popular among many Greeks.

Luke 6:27-38

After the beatitudes and the woes (6:17-26), Luke continues with Jesus' teaching on the qualities of a genuinely Christian attitude toward others (vv. 27-49). Today's reading includes the unit's first part, given in direct non-metaphorical form. The remainder (vv. 39-49) consists of related teaching and further developments in images.

The basic attitude inculcated in 6:27-35 is a love so disinterested that it refuses to differentiate between friend and enemy. Its test is precisely love of one's enemy. Not without paradox, Jesus teaches that selfless love will bring its author a reward as rich as it is unsought for (v. 35). The passage includes the golden rule (v. 31), a thumbnail criterion of universal application. Here it provides an experiential basis for the moral judgment that one should indeed love one's enemies. As someone else's enemy, Jesus' hearers would surely appreciate being loved.

The ultimate basis for love of enemies and selfless giving is theological. In loving, the Christian imitates God's goodness which does not distinguish between good and bad, but extends even to the ungrateful and wicked. Imitating God's attitude, Christians can rightly be called children of the Most High (v. 35). A genuine child of God truly reflects God's life and goodness. The reading concludes by applying the golden rule to various aspects of the Christian's practical attitude (vv. 36-38). Again Jesus alludes to our divine exemplar, but he reinforces the norm by enriching it with the notion of God's fatherhood (v. 36).

   1. The Christian notion of resurrection cannot be arrived at by philosophical reasoning but only through faith in God's action on our behalf (1 Corinthians 15:45-49).

   2. A paradox of selfless Christian love is that, while it seeks no reward, it is richly rewarded (Luke 6:35).

   3. The ultimate basis for undifferentiated love of friend and enemy is God's loving concern for all people (Luke 6:35-36).

Because the Eighth, Ninth and Tenth Sundays are not used liturgically, they are not included here.

Eleventh Sunday of the Year

Jesus offers reconciling grace to all, without respect for our degree of sinfulness. In Luke 7:36-8:3, we meet Jesus' welcoming gesture with gratitude, faith and love (7:36-50), and we join him in the mission (8:1-3). God's dealing with David helps us appreciate God's graciousness as well as the conditions for divine forgiveness (2 Samuel 12:7-10, 13). Through faith Christ lives in us and we are justified in his sight (Galatians 2:16, 19-21).

2 Samuel 12:7-10, 13

God's gift to David is recalled by the prophet Nathan (12:7-8), who contrasts what God has done for David with David's sinful behavior. David killed Uriah by placing him in a situation where he would be struck down by the warring Ammonites. By taking Uriah's wife, David has spurned the Lord (v. 9). His action has called forth divine punishment. Having killed by the sword, David's royal house would be ravaged by the sword (v. 10). This is the law of retributive justice.

Divine justice, however, is not without appeal. Repentance nullifies the offense in God's sight and is met with forgiveness. Accordingly, David confesses his sin (12:13a). His admission of guilt rectifies his stance before God and constitutes an implicit plea for forgiveness. Nathan is God's spokesman as he affirms divine forgiveness. Without repentance, David would have died like Uriah. Repentant, he shall live (12:13b).

Psalm 32:1-2, 5, 7, 11

Forgiveness should not be taken lightly. It calls for gratitude, and Psalm 32 helps us express it. In vv. 1-2 we join the psalmist in acknowledging the happy state of the forgiven person. After two "beatitudes," attention turns to the one praying. He is the happy one; he is forgiven because he has confessed his sin (v. 5). Because God is our shelter and protector (v. 7), we invite all the just to rejoice with us (v. 11). Having been forgiven in the past, the community asks for forgiveness in the future: "Lord, forgive the wrong I have done."

Galatians 2:16, 19-21

Paul is extremely displeased with the Galatians who have been returning to their pre-Christian state. They believed they were justified by fulfilling the law. At stake was the gospel itself, which transcended life under the law and provided a new principle of justification.

Faith, like the law, has concrete implications for personal and communal living. In 2:16, Paul does not contrast Christian faith with the living out of faith in deeds. Rather, he contrasts the status of Christians (faith) with their former state as Jews (the law and its works). For those who had heard the gospel, the only possible justification is through faith in Christ.

Paul and his readers had died to their former existence, including the law. In baptism, they died with Christ to live for God in an entirely new way (2:19). As a result, Christians now have a new principle which through faith infuses their human life with that of the Son of God (2:20). This gracious gift had been offered through Christ's death that others might live. When the Galatians return to the law, the condition of life that preceded Christ's crucifixion and their baptismal participation in it, they spurn and nullify God's saving work on our behalf.

Luke 7:36-8:3

The reading includes two units. The first is a story concerning Jesus' attitude toward a sinful woman (7:36-50). The second, an introduction to the gospel's next part, notes the growing number of those who accompany Jesus as he continues his itinerant mission (8:1-3).

Jesus is now a guest in a Pharisee's home (7:36). Earlier in the gospel he had been a tax collector's guest (5:29), and this had earned his disciples the reproach of Pharisees and scribes (5:30). In today's reading, a sinful woman enters the Pharisee's home. She had heard Jesus was present and came to anoint him in witness to her repentant love (7:37-38). The story is related to Mark 14:3-9. Its literary development and theological orientation, however, are typically Lukan. As in 5:30, the Pharisee reacts negatively to Jesus' reconciling acceptance of the sinner (7:39).

Jesus responds to the Pharisee's unspoken objection with a brief parable (7:40-43) to illustrate how forgiveness of a greater debt evokes greater gratitude. The Pharisee should consequently be able to understand the woman's extraordinary response.

In 7:44-47, Jesus addresses his host and contrasts the woman's behavior with the Pharisee's. Because she had loved much, much is forgiven her. Indirectly, the Pharisee is urged to greater love. In 7:48-50, Jesus addresses a forgiving word to the woman and presents the grounds of reconciliation. In forgiving, Jesus acknowledges the sinner's saving faith.

1. God's life-giving forgiveness is readily granted to those who repent (2 Samuel 12:7-10, 13).

2. Like Paul, we give human expression to the life of the Son of God (Galatians 2:16, 19-21).

3. Faith and love are the fundamental conditions for reconciliation at Jesus' table (Luke 7:36-50).

Twelfth Sunday of the Year

Suffering is inescapable. It was intimately related to Jesus' identity and mission (Luke 9:18-24) just as it had been related to Jerusalem's function in salvation history (Zechariah 12:10-11). The passion is an essential part of life for all who share Christ's divine sonship. They experience this especially in the concrete efforts to recognize the universality of salvation in Christ (Galatians 3:26-29).

Zechariah 12:10-11

Deutero-Zechariah (chapters 9-14) is divided into two parts (chapters 9-11; 12-14). Rich in messianic expectation (cf. 9:9ff), part one is a word of hope addressed to a people suffering at its rulers' hands (11:4-17). In part two, messianic expectation assumes apocalyptic overtones. Hope in God's deliverance is affirmed in the face of foreign assaults against Jerusalem.

Today's reading describes the mourning over Jerusalem whose destruction is compared to the death of an only child (12:10b-11). Jerusalem's destruction, however, is also an outpouring of a spirit of grace and petition on David's house and the city's inhabitants (12:10a). In 13:1, God's action is further described as the opening of a fountain to purify the people from sin and uncleanness.

Years later, this text would provide part of the biblical inspiration for interpreting the death of Christ the only son as a positive divine action for the forgiveness of sins. Deutero-Zechariah 12-14 represented an important theological effort to grasp the meaning of Jerusalem's passion in light of Israelite faith. Its theology and language provided a model for understanding Jesus' passion in light of Christian faith.

Psalm 63:2, 3-4, 5-6, 8-9

A great prayer formulates our yearning for God. The psalmist views himself as distant from the source of life and refreshment (v. 2). He gazes toward God's dwelling and recognizes God's kindness (vv. 3-4). He knows he will be able to bless God, an all-satisfying act (vv. 5-6). God helps those who joyfully cling to him (vv. 8-9). The assembly echoes the attitude forcefully expressed in the psalm's first verses: "My soul is thirsting for you, O Lord my God."

Galatians 3:26-29

By our faith in Christ Jesus, we are all God's children (v. 26) because Jesus Christ is Son of God. Our relationship to the Son, initiated by baptismal faith, has given each one a share in the Son's life so that with him we are God's children (v. 27a).

To express this, Paul drew a metaphor from ordinary life. People "put on" a garment (v. 27b). "Putting on Christ," however, can facilitate understanding only when used with other expressions of this same reality. By itself it is hardly adequate to describe the transforming union which transcends all ethnic (Jew, Greek), social (slave, free) or biological (male, female) distinctions among Christians. In Christ all are one (v. 28).

The purpose of Paul's discussion is to relate early Christian communities to their biblical origins. Since Christ was heir to the promise made to Abraham, all united to Christ share in Abraham's heritage (v. 29). Paul was responding to accusations that life in his communities was contrary to biblical tradition.

By eliminating distinctions among Christians, the Pauline communities were indeed innovative. Gentiles, slaves and women had been excluded from full membership in the synagogue. To make his point, Paul returns to the origins of biblical tradition in Abraham's life. His message continues to challenge all efforts at maintaining distinctions among Christians by excluding certain members from full participation in Christ's life and mission.

Luke 9:18-24

The matter of Jesus' identity is frequent in the gospels. Here, as in other instances, it is introduced in question form: who do people say that I am (v. 18)? From the answers (vv. 19-20), we note it is not a matter of identifying Jesus in terms of his parentage, ethnic origins or curriculum vitae, but in relation to his role in the history of God's dealings with humanity.

Some say he is John the Baptist, others Elijah, still others one of the old prophets risen from the dead (v. 19). Not that Jesus was mistaken for someone else, but the meaning of his work was equated with that of other figures, who did indeed help articulate Jesus' meaning. Jesus' role, however, transcended all these. As Peter proclaims in the name of the disciples who had joined Jesus at prayer (v. 18a), Jesus is the Christ of God, that is the messiah, God's chosen one, anointed to bring about Israel's redemption (v. 20).

Jesus' messianic role could be misinterpreted as a political, social function in human history. He consequently orders his identity not be divulged (v. 21). The imposed silence is related to his messianic mission to suffer, be rejected, killed and raised on the third day (v. 22). Failure to present him in this role would distort his messianic function. While verbally correct, Peter's confession was open to misinterpretation.

A proper interpretation of Jesus' messianic mission was imperative for his followers. They too would have to bear a cross. Unless they saw Christ's sufferings as meaningful, they could not grasp the significance of their own. The latter would be seen as contrary to Christ's historic achievement and would lead to defections from the community (vv. 24-25).

1. The love and dedication manifested in suffering over the destruction of what we love, or the pain of death of those we love, is a prayer calling God's peace down on us (Zechariah 12:10-11).

2. Every Christian without distinction is called to assume a full mission in the church's work (Galatians 3:26-29).

3. Whoever would assume a role in the Christian mission must, like Christ, be willing to accept suffering and difficulty as a condition for its fulfillment (Luke 9:18-24).

Thirteenth Sunday of the Year

Life is a journey, and Christian life is a journey with Christ. Our efforts and their reception are patterned on those of Jesus (Luke 9:51-62). As we embark on the way to full freedom (Galatians 5:1), we bid adieu to our past (1 Kings 19:16, 19-21). On our journey, we must be led by the Spirit and resist any temptation to return to the destructive safety of slavery (Galatians 5:13-18).

1 Kings 19:16, 19-21

Elisha's call, divinely ordered in 19:16, is narrated in 19:19-21. While Elisha was at work in the fields with a yoke of oxen, the prophet Elijah came to him and cast his cloak upon him (v. 19). The hair-shirt mantle was part of the prophet's traditional garb (2 Kings 1:8). The action signifies Elisha's investiture among the prophets. Since the mantle symbolized the bearer's person and rights, the gesture was also a call to join Elijah and eventually to succeed him in his prophetic mission.

Elisha's immediate response was a request to kiss his father and mother farewell. Granting the request, Elijah tells him something important has been done to him (v. 20). Elisha should leave his work, bid adieu to his parents and return to take up his new vocation. Elisha left the prophet, slaughtered the oxen, used the rest of his equipment as fuel for cooking, and provided his family with a farewell banquet. The text indicates that Elisha's prophetic call required a total break with his past. Leaving his parents, the young prophet rejoined Elijah and followed him as his attendant. Later he would succeed Elijah and fulfill the mission originally entrusted to the older prophet.

Centuries later, Elisha's call would influence the New Testament's interpretation of the call of the first disciples and of all called to Christ's following.

Psalm 16:1-2, 5, 7-8, 9-10, 11

A song of trust expresses faith in God's saving power. We affirm our concrete relationship to God (vv. 1-2, 5) and bless the Lord for his sustaining presence (vv. 7-8). Our trust is well-founded (vv. 9-10); in God's presence we are filled with joy (v. 11). As men and women still on the way, we proclaim, "You are my inheritance, O Lord."

Galatians 5:1, 13-18

Christ has set us free, but Christians can still return to the condition of slaves. Paul exhorts his readers to stand fast in their freedom (5:1). The need for this exhortation presupposes that, although freedom is highly prized, its cost and implications are great. For those already free, slavery may well appear the easier way. As evidence Paul had the developing situation in the Galatian community.

In vv. 13-18, Paul contrasts the way of freedom, that of the Spirit, with the way of slavery, that of the flesh. References to walking and being led stem from the ancient biblical imagery of the way, a symbol for conduct in life's historical movement. The term apt to cause the most difficulty, however, is flesh. The homilist must take care not to limit its meaning to the sexual sphere. For Paul, the flesh was everything within us that stands in opposition to God. The flesh, not the body, is caught in an inner struggle with the Spirit, symbol of our union with God. The body is our very self, capable of transcending even death.

To be led by the Spirit is to fulfill the commandment of love (v. 14), according to which Christians are called to serve one another (v. 13). Paul interprets the law of love in a Christian sense. Unlike Leviticus 19:18, where the neighbor was defined as an Israelite, Christian love must reach out to all without distinction (cf. Galatians 3:28, p. 106). Failure to live by the Christian law of love results in self-destruction, the flesh's victory (v. 15). Christians should make no mistake. The flesh is opposed to the Spirit (vv. 16-17). The Spirit transcends the old law's limitations and restrictions (v. 18).

Luke 9:51-62

The second part of Luke's narrative of Jesus' mission begins with 9:51. Jesus deliberately directs his steps toward Jerusalem, the place where he would be taken up. The events in Jerusalem are seen from the point of view of the ascension, Jesus' departure from history for God's right hand. Every event along the journey, obviously theological, becomes part of Jesus' movement to his post-historical destiny. Along the way Jesus teaches the disciples to join him in that journey. Having shared Jesus' life, they will later understand the meaning of his absence and courageously pursue the way Jesus had taught them.

Verses 52-56 relate the disciples to Jesus' journey. They are impatient at the poor reception they receive in the mission (v. 54). Jesus rebukes them (v. 55). Their lot will not be different from his, prefigured by his rejection in Samaria (v. 53). Rejected, they must simply pursue their mission in another place (v. 54). In Luke-Acts, persecution and rejection are consistently interpreted as an occasion for broadening the scope of the Christian mission.

In vv. 57-62, some of those whom Jesus meets on the way to Jerusalem ask to join him (vv. 57-58, 61-62) or are invited to do so (vv. 59-60). In three stages, Jesus sets out the demands of his way on those who would follow. Following Jesus requires detachment from the comfort of a permanent earthly home (v. 58), from preoccupation with what is dead and past (v. 60) and from any turning back to one's former relationships (v. 62). The proclamation of the kingdom calls for a way of life suited for the kingdom.

> *1. Like Elisha and the first disciples, we are called to join Christ in his prophetic mission. After a period of apprenticeship, we shall assume an important role in continuing Christ's mission beyond the limits imposed by his historical life (1 Kings 19:16, 19-21).*
>
> *2. Love is the only way to Christian fulfillment; failure to love destroys oneself and the community to which one belongs (Galatians 5:1, 13-18).*
>
> *3. Jesus' absence, effected by the ascension, is a necessary condition for assuming our role in the Christian mission and for understanding the pain of departure in all the small deaths that accompany the Christian on the way (Luke 9:51-62).*

Fourteenth Sunday of the Year

We belong to the vast crowds that through the centuries have joined Jesus on his journey to Jerusalem. In Luke 10:1-12, 17-20, the future church is symbolically represented by the 70. Isaiah 66:10-14 evokes Jerusalem rejoicing over her renewed life. Even as we rejoice in hope, however, we can never forget the cross through which hope will become reality (Galatians 6:14-18).

Isaiah 66:10-14

Deutero-Isaiah's last chapter opens with a song in which the prophet joyfully announces a purified Jerusalem's renewed life (66:1-16). The purification did not separate Jews from gentiles but the good from the evil. Understandably, the text was frequently quoted by Christians as they reflected on the association of Jews and gentiles in the early communities.

In Isaiah 66:10-14, the prophet invites all who love Jerusalem to rejoice with her. Until now their love was expressed in mourning (v. 10). Henceforth they are invited to draw nourishment from her and to drink of her glory. The images suggest the comforting warmth and intimacy to be enjoyed by the mourners (v. 11). Jerusalem's God-given prosperity is like an overflowing stream and will be shared with all her children.

In vv. 13-14, the role of consoler is transferred from Jerusalem to God. Although consolation and joy are realized through the people's association with Jerusalem, their source is actually God who manifests his love through earthly realities. In passages like this, we have an Old Testament background for the strong sense of sacramentality that pervades early Christianity.

Psalm 66:1-3, 4-5, 6-7, 16 and 20

Praise (vv. 1-12) and thanksgiving (vv. 13-20) are this psalm's themes. The immediate liturgical context is obvious. Verses 1-5 invite all on earth to praise God for everything he has done, in particular the extraordinary events of the exodus from Egypt (vv. 6-7). The psalmist publicly proclaims the deeds that call for thanksgiving (vv. 16, 20), and the community responds: "Let all the earth cry out to God with joy."

Galatians 6:14-18

In the letter's conclusion, Paul certifies its authenticity (6:11). He attributes the circumcision movement threatening the community to those who live according to the flesh (v. 12a; cf. last Sunday), and charges them with avoiding persecution for Christ's cross (v. 12b). They do not even keep the old law, now transcended by the law of the Spirit. Their only desire is to draw others to live according to the flesh. That is their vision of glory (v. 13).

For Paul, the only true glory is in Christ's cross. All including Paul have been crucified from the point of view of their fleshly relationships. Paul demonstrates his willingness to oppose the flesh wherever he sees its influence. He is ready to suffer the consequences of his action (v. 14). What matters is the new creation that transcends the circumcision of the Jews and the uncircumcision of the gentiles (v. 15).

The new creation is the result of the cross. Through it Christ entered into a new life which he shares with all. The new creation is the universal Israel of God, not the old Israel partly defined by its separation from the gentiles. To all who walk in God's Israel, Paul offers the peace and mercy of a new covenant (v. 16). Tired of this question, Paul asks that he no longer be troubled with it (v. 17). The letter ends with a final blessing (v. 18).

Luke 10:1-12, 17-20

The appointment and mission of the 70 marks a major expansion of the original disciples. Required by the vast mission for which there were too few apostles, they are sent to spread Jesus' work and message. They are asked to pray their own numbers be supplemented (v. 2). Sent two by two, they reflect a Christian adaptation of Jewish custom, according to which itinerant missionaries traveled in pairs (v. 1). Even John the Baptist had followed this custom (7:18).

The disciples' way would not be easy. On all sides they would be threatened like lambs among wolves (v. 3). In v. 4, we have a statement of the radical and single-minded nature of life on mission. For later communities, when the mission spread to the whole empire, these demands would be modified (22:35-36) because of the difficult challenges of the far-ranging mission.

The disciples' greeting is peace (vv. 5-6). They are to accept hospitality but without being demanding, taking whatever is offered them (vv. 7-8). They should heal the sick and proclaim the kingdom's imminence to those who receive them (v. 9). When rejected, they must leave the place, but not without indicating that the kingdom had been near. The town which rejects them shall be judged more harshly than ancient Sodom (vv. 10-12).

The disciples return from the mission with accounts of their success (v. 17). Jesus congratulates them (v. 18-19) but warns them to rejoice in their salvation, not in their success.

> *1. God manifests his love for us through the ordinary and extraordinary things around us (Isaiah 66:13-14).*

2. *Christ shares his new life with all; this calls for an attitude that respects and loves all men and women irrespective of accidental human differences (Galatians 6:14-18).*

3. *The early disciples' sense of mission must characterize all who follow Christ (Luke 10:1-12, 17-20).*

Fifteenth Sunday of the Year

Salvation is extremely close. Luke forbids us to evade the responsibility of loving our neighbor. The question is not "Who is our neighbor?" but "How are we to be good neighbors?" Salvation is through our attitude (Luke 10:25-37), transformed by God's immanent word (Deuteronomy 30:10-14). That word is made present in Christ, the center of both creation and history (Colossians 1:15-20).

Deuteronomy 30:10-14

Moses' farewell discourse to the Israelites is the major portion of the book of Deuteronomy. Writing long after Moses' death, the author invokes Moses' authority by having the lawgiver address the problems of a future time. In effect, the discourse articulates what Moses would say if he were alive. The book corresponds to the general purpose of farewell discourses in ancient literature.

Among the major problems faced by the Israelite community in the northern kingdom of Israel was temporal remoteness from the covenant and the events in which they found their origins. The author affirmed that the covenant and God's word are now. In Deuteronomy 30:9-10, Moses promises prosperity for all who obey God's word written in the book of the law, that is, Deuteronomy. The written word actualizes the ancient law in the present. Obedience to the law is a turning to God with all one's heart and soul.

Not only is the word *now*, it is also *near* (vv. 11-14). There is no need to seek it in heaven or beyond the seas. On the contrary, it is in the mouth and heart of the faithful. The actualization of the written word takes place through the reading, speaking and living of the law. Since the word has been internalized, it can be fulfilled. Theologically, the passage recalls Jeremiah 31:31-34, where the Lord promises that in the new covenant the word will be written in his people's hearts.

Psalm 69:14, 17, 30-31, 33-34, 36-37

A narrative of suffering and public reproach (vv. 1-13) is interrupted by a prayer (v. 14-19), in which the psalmist begs God for help (vv. 14, 17). An exclamatory prayer (v. 30) introduces anticipated thanksgiving for God's expected saving action (vv. 31-37). On this basis, the assembly urges all, "Turn to the Lord in your need, and you will live."

Colossians 1:15-20

The thanksgiving unit of Paul's letter to the Christians of Colossae (1:3-14) ended with a reference to the kingdom of the Father's beloved Son. In 1:15-20, Paul proceeds to describe the Son's meaning, role and exalted position in theological terms. In two subsequent units he describes the concrete situation of the Colossae Christians (vv. 21-23) and of himself (vv. 24-29; cf. next Sunday, p. 116) in relation to Christ the Son.

To appreciate Paul's Christology, recall the Old Testament's hymns in praise of wisdom, especially Wisdom 7 and Proverbs 8 (cf. p. 169). Colossians 1:15-20 was very likely an early Christological hymn based on wisdom reflection, which Paul incorporated into his letter.

Like wisdom, Christ is the invisible God's image and the firstborn of all creation, in whom all things were created. Christ is thus God's visible manifestation. By his relationship to creation, everything shares in the sacramental expression of God's invisible being. Since all things are related to him, he stands preeminent, the head of his body the church. She is reconciled with God by her relationship to Christ in whom God's fullness dwells.

In this theology, the world and its inhabitants are a new creation effected by God's work in Christ. The key to understanding is the view that divine wisdom can be incarnate and that wisdom binds all created reality into one.

Luke 10:25-37

A lawyer questions Jesus on what he must do to inherit eternal life (v. 25). Jesus responds with a question and leads the lawyer to provide the answer himself (vv. 26-27). It is in two Old Testament commandments, that join love of God (Deuteronomy 6:5) and love of neighbor and oneself (Leviticus 19:18). In Jesus' estimation, the lawyer's answer is correct. If he acts according to his word, he shall live (v. 28). This promise of life includes both historical existence and the afterlife. Without these two commandments, the lawyer would experience only death.

So simple a formula for life is not without its hidden agenda. Accordingly, the dialogue moves on to lay bare a major social question confronting first century Jews, their long-standing separation from the Samaritans. Asking a general question concerning his neighbor's identity, the lawyer sought to limit love's scope. By telling the story of the good Samaritan, however, Jesus broadened the scope, refusing to define the neighbor in terms of ethnic origins or religious adherence. The neighbor is everyone. The lawyer deserves the name neighbor only if he proves himself genuinely compassionate and merciful toward all (vv. 30-35).

Very subtly, Jesus has turned the question completely around to focus on the neighbor not as love's object but as the subject, the one who loves. The lawyer wanted to identify those persons whom he should love as his neighbor. Jesus forced him to think of himself as the neighbor in terms that transcended his Jewish birth and his standing in the community. As a member of the human community of God's people, he has to recognize all human beings as his neighbor.

1. Like the Israelites, the Christians' relationship to God is now, not merely a matter of past history (Deuteronomy 30:10-14).

2. In Christ, God's wisdom is expressed in relation to every aspect and challenge of human life (Colossians 1:15-20).

3. The real question is what we ourselves must do to be a Christian neighbor (Luke 10:25-37).

Sixteenth Sunday of the Year

Attention to guests through whom we hear Christ's word is an essential element in the liturgy. We recognize Martha's problem as ours and learn to shape our attitude (Luke 10:38-42). As a precedent, Abraham's marvelous sense of hospitality reveals the way to life (Genesis 18:1-10). Paul relates our life and role to Jesus the Lord (Colossians 1:24-28).

Genesis 18:1-10

The story of the Lord's appearance to Abraham by the oaks of Mamre (18:1-15) is one of the Old Testament's narrative gems. As Abraham sat at his tent door, dozing in the day's heat, he raised his eyes to see three men standing before him (vv. 1-2a). Abraham's daydream assumes vivid reality as he runs to meet them. Bowing to the earth in a traditional gesture of desert hospitality, the patriarch offers them water, washing for their tired feet, rest in the shade of his tree and a morsel of bread. Refreshed by one who deems himself their servant, they might then go on their way.

The visitors willingly accept (vv. 2b-5). With Sarah's help, Abraham prepares a marvelous banquet and sets it before them. He stands by in silence as they eat (vv. 6-8). The reader has to smile at Abraham's sumptuous fulfillment of his modest offer of a morsel.

For those who have enjoyed the hospitality of desert tribes in the Near East, the scene marvelously evokes a way of life where silence is a mode of respectful communication, where hospitality is a radical ethical demand and a fundamental expression of human dignity, and where the host is at the human service of his guest. This passage describes what a eucharistic celebration ought to be.

After the meal, silence is broken by the guests. Inquiring about Sarah and learning she is in the tent, they announce their return in spring. At that time Sarah shall have a son (vv. 9-10). At this point, the three men merge into one, and he is the Lord.

The promise of a son must be seen in the context of ancient hopes to transcend earthly existence through one's offspring. The promise to Abraham is a promise of immortality. Through Sarah's son, Abraham will become the father of a race which would one day be God's people.

Psalm 15:2-3, 3-4, 5

In v. 1, this psalm asks who shall participate in the Lord's liturgy. The verses selected for today's meditation provide the answer. What is required is blameless conduct, understood in relation to the law of charity, with important implications in the matter of wealth and poverty (vv. 2-5). "He who does justice will live in the presence of the Lord," is the community's response.

Colossians 1:24-28

Reflecting on his life, Paul places Christ's work (cf. last Sunday, p. 114) in historical perspective. Since Christ is the firstborn of all creation, he had in a sense played a limited role in history. Others would come after him, be united with him and share the life of the new Adam, just as they had enjoyed the life of the old Adam. These others would have significant, albeit relative, roles to play in history. In the way of Christ, they would help complete what was lacking in his afflictions. Indeed, by reason of his relationship to the church, Christ's life is not complete independently of his body. In this context Paul views his own sufferings (v. 24).

Like Christ, Paul's sufferings were for the church's benefit, an expression of the ministry he had received. He fulfilled this ministry by making God's word fully known (v. 26), that is, by drawing out its universal nature as a word to gentiles as well as to Jews (v. 27). Paul's efforts went into assuring the word would fulfill this promise (vv. 27-28), formerly hidden and mysterious (v. 26), now gloriously revealed (v. 27). The sufferings Paul encountered in carrying out his mission of the word shared in the value of the sufferings of Christ, whose mission climaxed in death. They contributed to filling what was lacking in Christ's personal passion.

Luke 10:38-42

The story of Martha and Mary is an important Lukan statement concerning Christian hospitality as exercised in the eucharistic meal.

Since Martha and Mary lived at Bethany near Jerusalem, the journey (v. 38) appears out of context. At this point in the gospel, Jesus is still quite far from the environs of the city. Luke's concern, however, is not with geography. Omitting mention of Bethany, he simply situates the story along the way to Jerusalem. The episode and its teaching are presented as an important aspect of the way of the Christian disciple, symbolically evoked by the geographical journey theme.

In Luke's account, Martha is the principal personage, and the main theme is the problem she addresses to Jesus. Taken up with the manifold duties of hospitality, busy preparing the table, Martha is upset. Her sister Mary, preferring to listen to Jesus' words, is not helping her (vv. 39-40). In reply, Jesus focuses on hospitality's essential element, personal attentiveness to the guest (vv. 41-42).

Addressed to the Christian community, the account is a significant statement concerning the hierarchy of values in eucharistic fellowship. The details of the meal and its celebration are secondary. Only one thing is required, that participants attend to Christ's person present in those gathered for the eucharist. The quality of the eucharist is not to be judged by the elaborateness of the meal but by the depth of personal communication with Christ.

1. Hospitality is a major characteristic of life in both the Old and New Testaments (Genesis 18:1-10).

2. *The suffering of Christians is a continuation of the self-offering that marked Christ's life (Colossians 1:24-28).*

3. *The most important thing in the celebration of the eucharist is attention to Christ's presence in those assembled for the meal (Luke 10:38-42).*

Seventeenth Sunday of the Year

Prayer expresses our Christian stance before God. From him we receive everything, with him we cooperate in the kingdom's development (Luke 11:1-13). In Genesis 18:20-32, we learn that God's gracious gift is limited only by our hesitation to ask. In liturgical context, our hesitations are equivalent to the limited way we live the challenge of our baptism (Colossians 2:12-14).

Genesis 18:20-32

Like human situations where one must verify a report before taking action, the Lord decides to visit Sodom and Gomorrah to see whether the outcry from these cities springs from real offenses (vv. 20-21). The Lord is once again identified with the three men who had visited Abraham (cf. preceding Sunday). Abraham had accompanied them along part of their way (18:16). Although the three proceed toward Sodom, Abraham remains in the Lord's presence (v. 22).

The text assumes that God's plan to destroy Sodom and Gomorrah has been communicated to Abraham. He initiates a bargaining session with the Lord. Will God destroy the righteous along with the wicked? Recall that Abraham's nephew, Lot, resides in Sodom with his family (cf. Genesis 13 and 19). Would God spare the place for 50 righteous? Is he not a just judge (vv. 23-25)? Receiving a favorable answer (v. 26), Abraham is emboldened to lower the number. Suppose there are 45? 40? 30? 20? Ten? Each time, the Lord responds to Abraham's petition (accompanied by mounting protestations of unworthiness) that he would indeed spare the city (vv. 26-32).

As we know from the following chapter, Sodom was destroyed. The story is a marvelous exploration of human desire to know the mystery of divine justice in relation to the death of the righteous. It is also an affirmation of the boldness that ought to characterize prayer. At story's end, we can ask if Abraham failed in his quest because he didn't summon the courage to ask for more.

Psalm 138:1-2, 2-3, 6-7, 7-8

Our meditative prayer expresses the gratitude and worship that must follow our petition (vv. 1-2). We can presuppose God answers our prayer (v. 3). From his exalted position, he has a kindly regard for the lowly and the troubled (vv. 6-7a). By answering our prayer, he fulfills his plans in our regard (vv. 7b-8). The assembly responds, "Lord, on the day I called for help, you answered me."

Colossians 2:12-14

Paul's theology of baptism (cf. also Romans 6:1-11) speaks of Christians united with Christ first in his death and burial and secondly in his resurrection. Romans emphasized the ultimate resurrection in the future. Colossians describes its beginnings and development from the moment of baptism.

To understand this theology, we must keep in mind the biblical symbolism of water and of the baptismal rite. The initiate descended into the water and rose from it. In the scriptures, water evokes a variety of experiential meanings. As a symbol of purification, it presupposes inner impurity; in this context, baptismal water would be a spiritual cleansing. Traditionally most Christians have understood their baptism in this sense. However, it bears no relationship to Paul's theology of baptism in Colossians and Romans.

As a refreshment, water presupposes spiritual thirst. Accordingly, baptismal water quenches thirst for those who make their way beneath the hot sun of life's desert. With the recent renewal, many Christians have come to view their baptism in this sense, but again it is totally foreign to Colossians 2:12-14 and Romans 6:1-11.

In Colossians 2:12-14, water is a symbol of the netherworld (*She'ol* or Hades), the place of death to which all eventually descended. To appreciate the symbol, read the magnificent psalm in the second chapter of Jonah, where the prophet sees himself about to be overwhelmed by the waters of death. The netherworld's watery depths were also closely associated with the primeval chaos out of which God created an orderly universe (cf. Genesis 1:1-2). The waters symbolized our destructive return to nothingness. In this context, baptismal water symbolizes our acceptance of death, an attitude made possible because death no longer constituted our ultimate destiny. Associated with Christ in death, we rise with him as a new creation.

Luke 11:1-13

John's disciples prayed with a formula that expressed their identity as a community of Jews following John. Jesus' disciples grew in the awareness of their specific identity as his followers. Moved by Jesus' prayerful act, they asked him to teach them a similar prayer (11:1). Jesus responded with the prayer that most adequately characterizes his followers (vv. 2-4). The Lord's prayer is an expression of our Christian identity as we stand before God. Its invocation and two short sets of petitions provide a simple summary of the entire gospel.

The prayer in Luke 11:2-4 is one of at least two traditional formulations. The other, popularized from antiquity by the liturgy, is in Matthew 6:9-13. While the two versions are closely parallel in form and wording, the Lukan tradition is considerably shorter. However, since each element implies the others, this brevity is not an impoverishment but a more succinct poetic form.

Each phrase is extremely rich and open to long elaboration. Accordingly, Luke chose to focus attention on the prayer for daily bread. The two parables that follow the prayer develop aspects of our need for nourishment and God's willingness to fill our need. The first parable emphasizes persistence in our prayer for bread and the foundations of hope that God will amply fill our hunger (vv. 5-9). The second develops the nature of God's response—he does not deceive but truly corresponds to our genuine need (vv. 10-13).

> *1. God's response to prayer is limited only by the limits we place on our prayer (Genesis 18:20-32).*
>
> *2. To understand our dying and rising with Christ in baptism, we must be sensitive to the water symbol in the ancient biblical context (Colossians 2:12-14).*
>
> *3. The Lord's prayer speaks our Christian identity before God (Luke 11:1-13).*

Eighteenth Sunday of the Year

> *Wealth is one of God's blessings, but it is insignificant in relation to eternal life. Failure to maintain a proper sense of values in its regard leads to conflict and injustice (Luke 12:13-21). Ecclesiastes 1:2; 2:21-23 helps us to reflect on the passing nature of all earthly goods. With Paul in Colossians 3:1-5, 9-11,*

*we reject the worship of created things and put to death all that
is earthly within us.*

Ecclesiastes 1:2; 2:21-23

"Vanity of vanities! All is vanity" (1:2). Thanks to *The Imitation of
Christ*, this quote has made its way into popular Christian culture. Few
know its origins in Ecclesiastes or Qoheleth, as the book is called in
Hebrew. Like many other quotations from Qoheleth, this one is generally
understood as a reflection on the transitory nature of created things.
Christians should focus their attention on the things not of this world
which God has in store for them in the afterlife. Qoheleth, however, has no
vision of afterlife, and his wisdom is a commentary on mortality.

Among biblical books, Qoheleth is singularly fatalistic. Nothing that
happens or that we do makes any difference. The meaning of things and
events is inscrutable. If God has a plan, we cannot discern it. Should not
someone benefit from his work, especially when he has labored with
wisdom and knowledge? And yet he may never do so, leaving all for others'
enjoyment (2:21). Our only reward is the pain and vexation of restless toil.
Surely then, all is vanity or emptiness (2:22-23).

Qoheleth writes in an age when many had lost life's sense of purpose.
Why was the book incorporated in the scriptures? Faced with a similar
appraisal of reality, others called for the destruction of all things. Placing
their hope in God alone, they looked to the day when he would re-create the
world in a meaningful way. Their approach is apocalyptic. Others would
strive for a divine knowledge disassociated from earthly life. Their effort is
gnostic.

Qoheleth's genius lay in refusing these escapist theologies. Accepting
what appeared to be meaningless as being from God, the author taught
that, in spite of everything, each one should live by the law or Torah. In its
realism, his message addresses people who for a time have lost their sense of
co-creatorship and participation in salvation history.

Psalm 95:1-2, 6-7, 8-9

A call to worship (vv. 1-2) introduces this celebration of God's royal
dominion. Repeating the call, we recognize ourselves as the sheep of his
pasture (vv. 6-7). Since God is our shepherd, we must hear his voice and not
harden our hearts as happened long ago in the desert (vv. 8-9). The
assembly focuses attention on these last verses: "If today you hear his voice,
harden not your hearts."

Colossians 3:1-5, 9-11

The reading's first part establishes the grounds for a Christian ethical attitude (3:1-4; cf. Easter, p. 63). In vv. 5-11, Paul describes the concrete behavior of those raised with Christ. The Colossian community's actual problems, not unlike those of other communities past and present, provide the point of departure for this development.

The Christians must put to death everything within them which is earthly, that is, contrary to their share in Christ's heavenly life. The death imagery implies that Paul associated various acts and attitudes with baptism's first phase in which Christians died with Christ. The Christians must consequently behave in a manner consistent with their baptism. Excluded are fornication, impurity, passion, evil desire, and covetousness. Paul views covetousness as a form of idolatry, the worship of earthly created goods instead of the creator who alone is to be worshipped (v. 5). In vv. 6-8, not included in today's reading, Paul contrasts the readers' pre-baptismal state with the demands of their new life in Christ.

Those who have assumed a new nature must not lie to one another. This would be directly contrary to the faith knowledge that develops in the baptized as they grow in the creator's image (vv. 9-10). Lying is an attack on the life of faith and the meaning of baptism. In addition, no ethnic or social distinctions must be made among community members. Christ is fully and equally present in all members (v. 11).

Luke 12:13-21

Luke has an interest in Jesus' teaching on the values that should permeate Christians' activities and characterize their outlook on life. In today's gospel, the author confronts the issue of wealth. The passage is especially appropriate since it counters a rather romanticized view of poverty which many have mistakenly founded on Luke's gospel.

The occasion for Jesus' teaching is a dispute between two brothers (v. 13). Refusing to be an arbiter in a matter of mere greed, Jesus turns to the crowd and addresses it on the question of possessions (vv. 14-15). Jesus does not berate wealth. He attacks a value system which sets up possessions as life's guarantor. For the meaning of "life," confer the 15th Sunday of the Year, p. 114. The possession of earthly goods is not the problem but their false valuation, resulting in greedy, inordinate efforts to accumulate them.

To illustrate his point, Jesus tells a parable about a rich man who set his hope for future life on an extraordinary harvest. God declared him a fool, and that very night he died, leaving all behind (vv. 16-20). Drawing out the implications, Jesus distinguishes between selfish wealth, which leaves one empty-handed at life's end, and genuine wealth in God's sight, a harvest for eternal life (v. 21). Luke advocates not poverty, but a proper sense of values. Both the materially rich and the poor should acquire spiritual wealth.

1. There are times when all seems meaningless. Even in these circumstances the tradition of Christ's law should support us (Ecclesiastes 1:2; 2:21-23).

2. It is not enough to be baptized. We must live according to the commitment made in baptism (Colossians 3:1-5, 9-11).

3. Wealth in itself is indifferent. To use it for good we must view it with a Christian sense of values (Luke 12:13-21).

Nineteenth Sunday of the Year

Christians must share their goods with the needy. In this matter, we must always be on our guard, reacting against the ready tendency to misuse this world's goods (Luke 12:32-48). We must have the attitude of the Israelites awaiting deliverance from Egypt (Wisdom 18:6-9). With the author of Hebrews we respond in faith to God's will (11:1-2, 8-19). Then we can act on Jesus' challenge.

Wisdom 18:6-9

The book's second part (11:2-19:22) aims to buttress the faith and hope of the large Jewish community in Alexandria during the first century B.C. The author recalls God's fidelity during the trials of the exodus. In five units he shows how God's wonders on Israel's behalf closely paralleled the plagues leveled against Egypt (see 18:8). Today's reading is from the fifth unit (18:5-19:22), in which the many life-giving actions of the exodus are contrasted with the Egyptians' death.

After an initial statement on Moses' rescue from the Nile and the drowning of the Egyptians in the Reed Sea (v. 5), the reading deals with the attitudes and actions of the faithful Israelites awaiting deliverance from Egypt.

The night (v. 6) is that of the death of the Egyptian firstborn (vv. 10-19). The Egyptians had learned in tormented dreams why they should suffer and die (v. 19). The Israelites, forefathers of the Jews, had also received advance warning (v. 6). This knowledge bolstered the Israelites' trust in God's promises and enabled them to look forward to divine deliverance (vv. 6-7). The Egyptians merely discovered why they suffered (v. 19). The author's concern with the problem of divine justice and retribution is obvious.

In v. 9, we have a description of the virtuous life of the devout in anticipation of the night of exodus. The Israelites offered sacrifices in secret, covenanted to keep the law, and shared blessing and dangers, even as they sang their songs of praise. The verse clearly sets out the proper behavior for Jews experiencing difficulty in first-century Egypt.

Psalm 33:1 and 12, 18-19, 20-22

God is creator as well as Lord of history. His munificence inspires us to share with the needy. We praise him and recognize how wonderfully we are blessed (vv. 1, 12). He delivers from death those who respect or fear him (vv. 18-19). May he ever fill our expectant longing (vv. 20-22). The assembly has good reason to declare, "Happy the people the Lord has chosen to be his own."

Hebrews 11:1-2, 8-19

The letter to the Hebrews is an early effort to strengthen the practical faith of the Christians of Alexandria and environs. Shaken by developments out of keeping with Christian faith-understanding, the readers are reminded of the incarnation's implications and its relationship to life under a covenant now transcended by Christ's work. Knowing these affirmations seem contradicted by experience, the author provided important reflections on faith's nature and value.

A general statement on faith's meaning introduces the passage (11:1). Faith bears on things for which we hope and cannot yet see. It is lived with sure confidence and conviction. Given this definition, the readers should recognize they are not in possession of those realities toward which faith sets its hope. Throughout chapter 11, the author shows how this faith governed the attitude of Israel's heroic leaders. For this faith they were approved by God (v. 2).

Skipping verses about creation and three great figures of Israel's primeval history (Abel, Enoch and Noah), the reading focuses on Abraham (vv. 8-19). Along with Isaac (v. 20), Jacob (v. 21), Joseph (v. 22), Moses' parents (v. 23), Moses himself (vv. 24-31) and many others (v. 32), Abraham's experience provided a witness (12:1), encouraging those who now endure trials (12:7) with eyes fixed on Jesus, the ultimate exemplar (12:2-4). Each stage in the story of Abraham and Sarah emphasizes their steady obedience as they responded to God's will, supported only by faith.

Luke 12:32-48

An immense crowd had gathered around Jesus (12:1a). Although aware of its presence (12:13), he begins by addressing his disciples (12:1b). Only in vv. 54-59 is his message directly to the crowds. Today's reading includes several important points in Jesus' teaching to the disciples.

Luke addressees seem to have been experiencing problems analogous to those confronted by Jesus in discussions with the first disciples. Fear brought on by internal difficulties and persecution had led many Christians to seek after earthly personal security. Verses 32-34 respond to this fear and urge Jesus' disciples to continue to share generously with the needy. Doing so, they shall receive the reward of the kingdom (see Acts 2:42-47; 4:32-35).

Verse 35 evokes the language of Exodus 12:11. Readiness is the attitude of those who have joined Jesus on his exodus (9:31). They persevere in his way after the master's departure while awaiting his return. At the table of the kingdom, Jesus will wait on his servants (vv. 36-40; see Luke 22:24-30). For this, however, they must now be wide-awake and on their guard (vv. 37, 39-40; see 22:39-46).

From Peter's question in v. 41, we may assume the Christian communities addressed by Luke had difficulty including themselves among Jesus' addressees. Jesus' message is for everyone, but some have a greater responsibility in its fulfillment (vv. 47-48). At the master's return, those who oversee the community and dispense its goods according to need will be dealt with very severely if they fail to serve. The communities' problems are most sharply presented in v. 45.

1. *The Israelites of the exodus provide a model attitude for Christians who struggle to keep the new law in alien circumstances (Wisdom 18:6-9).*

2. *Supported by past experience, the Christian faith enables us to be open to the future and courageously to accept its challenges (Hebrews 11:1-2, 8-19).*

3. *Those entrusted with responsibilities in the Christian*

community must remember their stewardship and not use their position for selfish advantage (Luke 12:32-48).

Twentieth Sunday of the Year

Because all do not accept the Christian message of peace, it is paradoxically the occasion for discord. Luke asks us to face this reality (12:49-53). We cannot expect to be treated more gently than Jesus or the prophets before him. Among these, the liturgy evokes Jeremiah (Jeremiah 38:4-6, 8-10). Hebrews encourages us by graphically presenting the outcome of Jesus' acceptance of the cross (12:1-4).

Jeremiah 38:4-6, 8-10

Confined to the quarters of the palace guard (37:21), Jeremiah was far from silenced. At the beginning of Nebuchadnezzar's siege of Jerusalem, the prophet had spoken out concerning the approaching destruction (21:3-10). Imprisonment had done nothing to change his message (vv. 2-3; compare 21:8-10).

In today's reading, the princes of Judah take new action against Jeremiah (v. 4). Their motive is that his message of doom is demoralizing the soldiers and the people. The prophet's word was seen as contrary to the common good. Acceding to the princes' request, king Zedekiah placed Jeremiah in their power, and they threw him into a waterless but miry cistern (vv. 5-6). A Cushite (Ethiopian) with a high position at court interceded on Jeremiah's behalf. He was taken from the cistern and saved from death (vv. 7-10).

This episode from Jeremiah's life shows the risk taken by one who spoke prophetically. In the liturgy, it provides an Old Testament pattern for understanding Jesus' prophetic activity. Casting Jeremiah into the cistern symbolizes Jesus' baptism or death. Drawn from the cistern that he might live, Jeremiah liturgically symbolizes Jesus' emergence to risen life.

Psalm 40:2, 3, 4, 18

Verses from a psalm of thanksgiving (vv. 1-11) and lament (vv. 12-17) articulate our grateful recognition of what God has done for us (vv. 2-4) and express our prayerful expectation (v. 18). God has heard our prayer (vv. 2, 3a), given us life (v. 3b) and led us to sing a trusting song (v. 4). He has not forgotten us in our poverty (v. 18). The assembly prays, "Lord, come to my aid."

Hebrews 12:1-4

To appreciate today's reading, situate it in the context already set out in chapter 11 (see p. 124). Our faith is grounded on the witness of the great biblical figures whom God approved. Given their experience, we ought to be moved to persevere in our life's race, putting aside every encumbrance of sin (12:1). These examples of biblical faith are not foreign to us, because we belong to a new stage of the same history governed by God's providential plans. Indeed, biblical history is completed only in us (11:40), inspired by the example of Jesus who perfects our faith (12:2a). The author had already set out his historical synthesis in the book's introduction (1:1-4).

The cross was not a glorious or enjoyable prospect, but clearly a source of great shame. If Jesus endured it, it was for the sake of future joy, a hope well rewarded, since he subsequently took his place at the right of God's throne (v. 2b). We also have Jesus' life-long example. Opposition never brought despondency or led to abandonment of the struggle his mission entailed (v. 3). Christians should note their lot is not so demanding as Jesus'. No one has yet been called to resist the opposition of sinners to the point of having to die (v. 4).

Called forth by a critical situation in the life of the community, these reflections constitute an extremely clear and realistic statement on Christ's humanity. The author's argument makes no sense unless we can accept Jesus' historical life as human. Jesus' struggle with evil, his sufferings, his perseverance and his death were as real and difficult as they would have been for any of us.

Luke 12:49-53

The last portion of Jesus' message to the disciples in chapter 12 invokes apocalyptic imagery to describe his role in history. Jesus' lighting of a fire on the earth (v. 49) had been announced by John the Baptist (3:16-17). Judging and refining the Christian communities, Jesus' fire purifies those intended for the kingdom.

Verse 50 presents Jesus' approaching passion and death as a baptism. In the ancient biblical context, water was seen not only as life's refreshment but also as the symbol of death and the netherworld. Dying was sometimes figuratively described as a plunging into the depths of the waters (see Jonah 2 and Psalm 124:4-5). For John the Baptist's followers and the early

Christians, who were baptized by stepping into the waters, the death symbolism of water served to articulate baptism's meaning as a dying to one's former sinful self. In turn, baptism could then be used as an image for death, as in Jesus' present saying.

Verses 51-53 develop the social implications of Jesus' purifying action (v. 49) concretely effected in his passion and death (v. 50). Peace had been announced (Luke 1:79), already given on a special occasion (7:50), and consequently expected as the fruit of Jesus' mission (v. 51). Jesus' peace, however, would be granted only to the repentant (7:36-50). It would consequently be a major cause of division among those who may have been close to one another but who would now be divided in their relationship to Christ (vv. 52-53).

> *1. Those who speak prophetically must be willing to accept opposition; ultimately God will rescue them from death but not necessarily from physical death (Jeremiah 38:4-6, 8-10).*
>
> *2. Christians must look to Jesus as a man of faith. His faith was supremely rewarded to his benefit and ours (Hebrews 12:1-4).*
>
> *3. Jesus' peace does not gloss over human and religious differences; it is given in response to our commitment to him and may consequently separate us from people close to us (Luke 12:51-53).*

Twenty-first Sunday of the Year

> *Descent from Abraham did not guarantee salvation. Nor was it enough to have been in Jesus' company. Salvation comes when we take up his way to Jerusalem (Luke 12:22-30), a way open to all, as foreseen by Isaiah's perception of Israel's role in history (Isaiah 66:18-21). In a sense, Jesus' way can be compared to a race, for which we must train; but the goal stands sharply before us (Hebrews 12:5-7, 11-13).*

Isaiah 66:18-21

Along with 66:17, the reading constitutes the only prose unit in Trito-Isaiah (chapters 56-66). With 66:22-24, it forms the conclusion of the Isaiah work. Its message emphasizes the universality that characterizes this book, beginning especially with chapter 40.

The Lord will gather nations of every language to come to Jerusalem and see his glory (v. 18). To accomplish this, the Lord will set a sign among the nations (v. 19a). This sign is most probably a reference to the Jews of the diaspora, scattered throughout the world as seen by the prophet and his contemporaries. Geographically the nations include the lands from southern Spain (Tarshish) to the Ionian islands (Javon), from Africa (Put and Lud) to the Black Sea region (Tubal). The identification of Mosoch is unknown. Making his universal intention extremely clear, the author includes a vague reference to the distant coastlands which have never heard of the Lord.

The people, fugitives from Jerusalem, would one day return. The gentiles among whom they live would bring them as they themselves came to the city (v. 20). The text dramatizes vividly the vast movement of populations to God by listing every available means of travel and conveyance. Like the Israelites, the nations would bring their offering to the Lord in clean vessels (v. 20b). The distinction between clean and unclean would no longer apply. The reading prepares us for the strong universal note in today's gospel, where salvation is said not to depend on a physical relationship to Abraham.

Psalm 117:1, 2

Our meditation includes both verses of this brief psalm, a doxology. Verse 1 calls all the nations to praise the Lord. Verse 2 indicates the grounds for this praise. The assembly's response is from Mark 16:15, "Go out to all the world and tell the Good News."

Hebrews 12:5-7, 11-13

Having adduced Old Testament figures and Jesus as exemplars of the persevering faith with which Christians are now being challenged (see pp. 124, 127), the author buttresses his arguments with further considerations. Like earthly fathers, God our Father must also discipline his children (12:7). The scriptures say as much in the book of Proverbs 3:11-12. Discipline and reproof are not to be despised; nor should they prove disheartening, since they are an expression of God's love (vv. 5-6). The difficulties now endured by the community should be viewed positively as an encouragement.

In vv. 8-10, omitted from today's reading, the author affirms that accepting God's discipline is a sign and condition of genuine sonship (v. 8). Moreover, there is a major difference between the discipline meted out by an earthly father and that of our heavenly Father. The former prepared us for the life we now live, the latter for our future share in God's immortal life (vv. 9-10). Both sources of dicipline, however, are first experienced as unpleasant. Only later can they be appreciated as we enjoy the peace and justice for which they trained us (v. 11).

At this point, the author returns to the image of the race introduced in 12:1. Given the previous arguments (11:1-12:11), the Christians should adopt a resolute, disciplined attitude as they pursue their race on life's path, intent on the goal when all pain will be healed (vv. 12-13). Jesus himself had run a similar race (12:1-3).

Luke 12:22-30

At the beginning of this unit, the author recalls a major thematic thread joining the various elements of Jesus' teaching: his itinerant journey through the cities and towns on the way to Jerusalem (v. 22), the city of his exodus and the city of salvation. This explicit mention of Jerusalem serves as a good introduction for the question concerning who will be saved (v. 23).

Jesus' response invokes the stylistic device of hyperbole—the narrow door (v. 24)—whose purpose is to shock the hearers into awareness of their responsibility and to sensitize them to live in such a way that they will indeed be saved. Once their personal history on earth is over, it will be too late. Jesus will recognize only those who have followed his way, patterned on his journey to Jerusalem. At that time they might object that they had dined at his table (v. 25) and that he had taught in their streets (v. 26), but to no avail (v. 27).

Salvation is not automatic. It calls for a genuine acceptance of Jesus as he reaches out to men and women at table fellowship. The acceptance requires a correlative reaching out to Jesus. Further, it is not enough to have lived in the same social context in which Jesus taught. We must respond to his teaching by engaging in his way of life, otherwise he will not know our origins and he will ultimately reject us.

Verses 28-30 address the problem of the salvation of Jesus' own people, the Jews. Their fathers, Abraham, Isaac and Jacob and the prophets will have entered into God's kingdom, but Jesus' addressees will be rejected unless they heed his word. It is not enough to be a physical child of Abraham (3:8; 19:9); only repentant persons are true offspring of Abraham, and these include gentiles who will come from the ends of the earth.

1. *The Lord's universal offer of salvation implies a funda-*

mental solidarity among all human beings and a call for mu-
tual assistance as we make our way to God's dwelling (Isaiah
66:18-21).

2. Life is a school in which we are disciplined and taught to
share in God's immortal life (Hebrews 12:5-7, 11-13).

3. To be saved, we must respond to Jesus' reaching out to us
(Luke 12:22-30).

Twenty-second Sunday of the Year

Humility and generosity characterize those who gather at
Jesus' table. Since Christians are both guests and hosts at the
eucharistic assembly, Luke's message to take the lowest place
and to invite the stranger and the outcast is addressed to us
(Luke 14:1, 7-14). The necessary attitudes are developed in
Sirach 3:17-18, 20, 28-29. In the present liturgical context,
Hebrews' exhortation to perseverance is focused on the same
attitudes and behavior (Hebrews 12:18-19, 22-24).

Sirach 3:17-18, 20, 28-29

The book of Sirach, named after its author, Jesus, son of Eleazar, son of Sirach (50:27), records the wisdom of a Jerusalemite living in the first quarter of the second century B.C. Today's reading includes maxims dealing with humility (vv. 17-18), human efforts (v. 20), appreciation of wise proverbs (v. 28) and almsgiving (v. 29).

Humility is the standard of wise conduct. Its reward is a love which surpasses even that received in response to gifts (v. 17). The greater a person is, the more humble he must be. This is not only true in ordinary human affairs; a great person who is commensurately humble wins favor with God (v. 18). One should not strive after what surpasses human limitations or seek to know matters which lie beyond one's personal strength (v. 20).

A wise person can appreciate proverbs, and rejoices when someone listens attentively to his sayings (v. 28). Their truth can be verified only from experience. The sage has learned it from his own experience. He shares it with the young. If they accept its challenge, they too can gradually appreciate its truth from their experience. This is true of the above proverbs as well as of others, including the one that follows: alms atone for sins just as water quenches fire (v. 29).

Psalm 68:4-5, 6-7, 10-11

A call to celebration (vv. 4-5) is followed by a description of God as father of the fatherless and provider for the homeless (vv. 6-7). The meditation concludes with a reflection on how God fulfilled his loving role in the past (vv. 10-11). The psalm echoes the attitudes in today's readings. The assembly's response, "God, in your goodness, you have made a home for the poor," recognizes the Christian obligation to imitate God.

Hebrews 12:18-19, 22-24

In Hebrews 12:18-29, the author concludes the exhortation to perseverance in faith begun in 11:1. The verses for today's reading include the basic points. This final argument contrasts Christians' present experience with that of their biblical forebears. Several phrases emphasize the terrifying manifestation of God's presence to his people at Sinai (vv. 18-19). The Christians, on the other hand, approach God on Zion, the heavenly city where they draw near to the angels, to God, to the spirits of the just and to Jesus their mediator through whose blood they now live in a new covenant (vv. 22-24).

To the Israelites, God spoke on earth; to the Christians he spoke from heaven (v. 25). Remote from the early Israelite's experience, the author interprets the ancient biblical language of Exodus quite literally. He does this to make his main points: 1) although the Christians' lot is easier, the heavenly origin of God's word brings with it a great responsibility to persevere; 2) the Christians' race may be inspired by Jesus and their goal may be a share in his own achievement, but failure to persevere will also bring with it a greater punishment.

Even if we do not follow the author in his interpretation of the Sinai events, the difference between the symbolic language used to describe Sinai and Zion, as well as the contrast between Israelite emphasis on God's transcendence and the greater Christian experience of his immanence, make these verses a powerful message for modern Christians.

Luke 14:1, 7-14

Luke's chapter 14 presents Jesus' teaching on a number of questions regarding Jewish law (vv. 2-6), table fellowship (vv. 7-24) and discipleship (vv. 25-35). The setting is a sabbath meal in the house of a leading Pharisee (v. 1). Today's reading includes a parable (vv. 7-11) and indications regarding who is to be invited to the Lord's table (vv. 12-14).

The parable is addressed to the invited guests to counter their efforts to seek places of honor (v. 7). Its teaching complements Jesus' message to the community leaders in 22:24-30. The attitude required is unassuming humility. Those who take a humble position with no thought of self-aggrandizement will be elevated at the meal's fulfillment in God's kingdom (v. 15). Those who seek to be exalted will suffer shame at being lowered in the kingdom. At issue is the proper Christian attitude and the genuine source of human value among Christians. Having identified with the guests in the parable, the readers should grasp Jesus' one-line general application (v. 11).

Jesus then addresses the host concerning whom he should invite to dinner (v. 12a). His teaching bears on the social standing of those invited as well as on the attitude of the host who is responsible for inviting the guests. The criterion determining the guest list should not be human friendship, blood relationship or social standing. These invitations could amount to mere self-seeking (v. 12b). The Christian criterion transcends all natural ties and affinities and directly counters any attitude that would serve the host or enhance his social position (vv. 13-14).

Jesus teaching, both to guests and hosts, is part of the story of the background for the Lord's supper and is related to the meaning of true eucharistic fellowship.

1. It is true human actions can only be verified by experience, but we should pay close attention to the accumulated wisdom of those who experienced life before us (Sirach 3:28).

2. The intimacy with which God enters into the life of Christians brings with it a greater responsibility to respond and persevere in faith (Hebrews 12:18-19, 22-24).

3. Jesus' teaching lets us place ourselves alongside other Christians invited to the Lord's supper as well as relate to the many who appear humanly unrelated to us (Luke 14:1, 7-14).

Twenty-third Sunday of the Year

The kingdom's demands are radical. All relationships and possessions are relativized by the way of the cross (Luke 14:25-33). A prayer ascribed to Solomon prepares us to place all earthly things, including our bodies, in proper perspective (Wisdom 9:13-18). In Paul's letter to Philemon, we also learn how to view the earthly condition in Christian categories (Philemon 9-10, 12-17).

Wisdom 9:13-18

The book of Wisdom was written at Alexandria early in the first century B.C. when that city's large Jewish community was shaken by persecution and defections. Its purpose was to encourage and edify the Jews by reflecting on Israel's religious history in a manner appropriate to the challenges posed by Hellenistic Alexandria.

In Israelite and Jewish tradition, Solomon's name is associated with Wisdom just as the names of Moses and David are inseparable from the law and the psalms. In the book's second section (6:22-11:1), the royal sage speaks in praise of wisdom (6:22-8:21) and concludes with a long prayer that this wisdom be granted to Solomon so that through it he might know the divine pleasure (9:1-11:1).

Today's reading is from this prayer. It is difficult to see how the course of events expresses God's will (vv. 13-14, 15). This is due to the present human condition in which the mind is burdened by the corruptible body (v. 15). In this, the imprint of Plato's view of the human person, influential in shaping the Alexandrian intellectual milieu, is unmistakable. However, even in this life we are not without hope, for God's gift of wisdom, wherever granted, had enabled people to discern the straight path of God's will (vv. 17-18).

The wisdom in question is not the Platonic ideal but the ancient wisdom of Israel, granted by the merciful God of our fathers (9:1) to Solomon as an answer to prayer, just as it had been granted to the ancestors of the Jews.

Psalm 90:3-4, 5-6, 12-13, 14-17

With a prayer for help in adversity, a communal lament, we place earthly things and time itself in perspective (vv. 3-6). We pray for wisdom in understanding what we have just perceived (vv. 12-13) and ask for an abundance of God's gracious gifts (vv. 14-17). "In every age, O Lord, you have been our refuge," is the community response.

Philemon 9-10, 12-17

Philemon is the shortest of Paul's letters, the only one addressed to an individual not the leader of a Christian community. Philemon was a Christian of means in the community at Colossae. This personal one-chapter missive, written on behalf of Philemon's runaway slave Onesimus, was very likely sent around the year 62 when Paul also wrote the letter to the Colossians. As the most personal of Paul's letters, the note reveals the author's delicate astuteness in arguing on another's behalf. To be appreciated it should be read in its entirety. In fact, its brevity, 25 verses, furnishes an excellent opportunity for providing the liturgical assembly with the flavor of an entire Pauline letter.

Onesimus was not a Christian at the time of running away. However, he had come in contact with Paul, in prison at the time, and had been received by Paul (begotten) into the Christian community (v. 10). Paul is now sending back Onesimus, whose name means "useful," to Philemon, with the indication that Onesimus, formerly *useless*, would now be truly *useful* (vv. 11-12).

Appealing to Philemon on Onesimus' behalf, Paul argues not from right but from love (v. 9), from the Christian solidarity that binds all Christians into fellowship, and allows one member to represent another in the widely separated regions of the gospel ministry (v. 13). As a member of the community, Onesimus should be granted the same welcome that would be accorded the one who sent him, in this case Paul (v. 17).

Out of respect for Christian freedom, Paul refused to keep Onesimus without Philemon's consent (v. 14). Upon returning, the human slave will also be the master's Christian brother and their formerly temporal relationship will be eternal. Unless Onesimus had run away, none of this would have happened. Such is God's providence (vv. 15-16)!

Luke 14:25-33

Luke 14:1-24 presents a meal in the house of a leading Pharisee. During the meal, Jesus challenged the lawyers and Pharisees (vv. 3-6), the guests (vv. 7-11) and the host (vv. 12-24). Addressing the host with a parable, he described a dinner to which all would be invited (vv. 21-23). This theme of universality provides the literary context for today's reading in which Jesus addresses the crowd. The structural technique in which various categories of hearers are successively addressed appears several times in the gospel. John 'the Baptist's message (Luke 3:7-18) provides an excellent example.

The unit's link with 14:1-24 and 15:1-32 shows table fellowship continues to provide the theological setting for 14:25-35. For narrative reasons, however, the account moves physically away from the meal to introduce the crowds which have joined Jesus in his journey to Jerusalem (v. 25).

After a brief introduction (v. 25), we have two sayings of Jesus. The first deals with family relationships (v. 26) and the second with the Christian way of the cross (v. 27). These are joined to a third saying concerning possessions (v. 33) by two parables (vv. 28-30, 31-32), which show the author intends to describe what is necessary at the outset if one is to follow Jesus to the journey's end.

To grasp Jesus' teaching we must recall Luke 9:23-24, where taking up the cross and losing one's life are given as conditions for achieving salvation. By the same token, family and possessions must first be given up for them to acquire new meaning and value in the Christian context. Consequently, the issue is not one of abandoning all natural relationships, but of placing them in perspective and discovering their true value in light of Christian discipleship.

> *1. Our Christian relationship to each other transcends every human consideration that divides us socially (Philemon 9-10, 12-17).*
>
> *2. The gospel does not dispense us from using natural wit and charitable shrewdness in our relationships with each other (Philemon 9-10, 12-17).*
>
> *3. By turning to Christ, we discover a new Christian relationship to our family and possessions as well as to ourselves (Luke 14:25-33).*

Twenty-fourth Sunday of the Year

> *Christians must rejoice when those lost or dead are found and come to life. Three parables help us to focus on this challenge, which affects our whole approach to eucharist (Luke 15:1-32). In Exodus 32:7-11, 13-14, Israel abandons the pure worship of the Lord and becomes a prodigal. As a persecutor, Paul had been the same. However, we rejoice with him over his conversion to Christ and the Christian mission (1 Timothy 1:12-17).*

Exodus 32:7-11, 13-14

This second of the books that comprise the Pentateuch begins the story of Moses and his achievement, which is then pursued to the end of Deuteronomy and the narrative of his death. In its present form, Exodus reflects several centuries of writing, incorporating the work of the Yahwist (tenth and ninth centuries), the Elohist (eighth century) and the priestly school of writing (sixth and fifth centuries).

Today's reading is from the book's most ancient strand. At the peak of Israel's worldly history, when Solomon's court represented considerable political power, breadth of culture and a heady sense of achievement, the writer leads Israel to reflect on the temptation of apostasy by retelling the story of the golden calf.

Rich in the recent experience of Sinai, in the life of the newly-established covenant and in the possession of a law, the Israelites had succumbed to the temptation of reducing God to a golden representation and corrupting his worship with pagan practices.

A similar temptation now faced the Israelites. Rich in gold and distracted by the accoutrements of human wealth, they were distorting the religion shaped by Moses in the crucible of the exodus. The problem was not the abandoning of Israelite worship for paganism. They were allowing Canaanite rites to influence their view of God as the Lord of history, freely present to them and in no way controllable by ritual actions. Even less could he be praised by the orgiastic practices of the Canaanite religion that continued to surround Israel.

Psalm 51:3-4, 12-13, 17, 19

The assembly responds to a prayer for healing redemption with a phrase from the parable of the prodigal: "I will rise and go to my father" (Luke 15:18). We pray for cleansing mercy (vv. 3-4), for a new heart that will allow us to stand in God's presence (vv. 12-13) and for the grace to proclaim God's praises in contrite humility (vv. 17, 19).

1 Timothy 1:12-17

The New Testament includes three Pauline letters to individuals who were heads of Christian communities—the first and second to Timothy and the letter to Titus—the so-called Pastoral Letters. Whether these letters were actually written by Paul or drafted at a later time, on the basis of historical reminiscences of Paul's life and teaching, remains unclear.

The letters could have been written as late as the early second century to invoke Paul's authority in shaping the Christian leadership. The names Timothy and Titus, both of whom had been Paul's colleagues, would thus flow from the literary nature of these letters intended for a wider readership. It is not impossible, however, that Paul himself wrote the letters through a secretary toward the end of his life around 67. In either case, the relationship between Paul and his co-workers serves as an excellent point of departure for all now confronted with new problems in the church's life.

A principal concern in 1 Timothy, as in the other Pastoral Letters, is the leaders' behavior in the early churches. This area influenced today's reading in which Paul's life experience and attitudes are given as a model for his addressees.

Paul acknowledges his indebtedness and expresses his gratitude to Christ for the strength and fidelity which are his as Christ's servant (v. 12). He describes his pre-Christian life as a persecutor (v. 13) and indicates how he was subsequently graced (v. 14). In vv. 15-16, he situates his case in a broader reflection on Christ's work for sinners. The reflection leads to an exuberant word of praise (v. 17), most likely drawn from an early Christian hymn.

Luke 15:1-32

For background to 15:1-3, 11-32 see p. 51. After addressing various categories about the demands made by the sharing in Jesus' meal on the way (14:1-15), the author responds to a major problem. The Pharisees and the scribes cannot understand that Jesus would show solidarity with sinners by eating with them (15:1-2). Confronting this problem, Jesus speaks three parables: the lost sheep (vv. 4-7), the lost coin (vv. 8-10) and the lost (or prodigal) son (vv. 11-32).

In each parable, the author's emphasis is the sinner's repentance. Being found by Jesus and admitted to his table does not consist in a one-way action or relationship in which the sinner is passive. From the sinner's point of view, the acceptance of Jesus' hospitality is equivalent to repentance.

To understand Luke's message, we must then keep in mind that table fellowship implies reciprocity in the participants. Not only does Jesus show solidarity with sinners, but sinners who join him at table manifest their acceptance and solidarity with him. Otherwise they would not be able to be with him at table. By sharing with Jesus at a meal, sinners join him in his values and attitudes. In other words, they manifest repentance in a positive way and can no longer be regarded as sinners.

1. The temptation to reduce God to a manageable idol, and worship to a pagan self-serving exercise is still alive (Exodus 32:7-11, 13-14).

2. Paul's passage from pre-Christian life to graced apostle-

ship is reflected in our development out of pre-Christian awareness to Christian commitment (1 Timothy 1:12-17).

   3. By joining the Lord's table, we accept his reconciling
gesture. But we also commit ourselves to his life values (Luke
15:1-32).

Twenty-fifth Sunday of the Year

   *The enterprising sinner provides a lesson for Jesus' follow-
ers. We must learn to deal with the insecurity of earthly possessions and share generously with those in need (Luke 16:1-13).
With Amos, we stand firmly against unjust socio-economic
oppression (8:4-7). Those in political authority need our prayers to fulfill their responsibilities before God and people (1
Timothy 2:1-8).*

Amos 8:4-7

   The book of Amos opens with a series of divine indictments against the
nations surrounding Judah and Israel. Six oracles against Aram (Damas-
cus), Philistia, Tyre, Edom, Ammon and Moab (1:3-2:3) are followed by a
denunciation of the southern kingdom of Judah (2:4-5). They climax in a
long, sweeping judgment of the northern kingdom of Israel (2:6-16).
Originating from Tekoa on the crest of the Judean hills, the shepherd-
prophet exercised his prophetic activity at Bethel, one of the ancient
shrines of the northern kingdom, during the reign of Jeroboam II (786-746
B.C.).

   At this time, a few years before the kingdom was conquered by Assyria
(721 B.C.), the northern kingdom had reached a high point of prosperity.
Wealth, however, was in the hands of a few and the majority suffered from
grave social injustice. Sensitive to the poor and weak, the prophet emerged
as a bold spokesman for social reform. He knew both sides because Amos
the shepherd was also a considerable merchant of the sheep he raised. As we
might expect, King Jeroboam and Amaziah, the wealthy priest of Bethel,
did not view Amos' efforts kindly. On the priest's initiative, Amos was
forced to leave Bethel and return to his native Judah (7:10-13).

   Today's reading is from the book's concluding section (7:1-9:15), which
presents two visions, in which God's punishing judgment is reversed by
the prophet's prayer (7:1-6), and three other visions whose threat will be
carried out (7:7-9:8a) but not without a promise of restoration (9:8b-15).

The unjust rich are addressed in strongly judgmental terms (8:4). However, the prophet does not himself describe their injustice. By an extremely effective literary device, he quotes his addressees as they hypocritically await the sabbath's end (8:5a) that they might cheat the poor and buy them into slavery (8:5b-6). The reading concludes with a statement that God will never forget what they have done (8:7).

Psalm 113:1-2, 4-6, 7-8

God helps the humble poor. With Psalm 113, we praise him for this and call upon all his servants to join us in blessing his name (vv. 1-2). No one equals his sovereign dominion and exalted position (vv. 4-6). This helps us appreciate his gracious gesture on behalf of the lowly (vv. 7-8). "Praise the Lord who lifts up the poor," is the communal response.

1 Timothy 2:1-8

Announced in 1 Timothy 1:18-20, Paul's solemn instructions for Timothy begin with today's reading. The entire section deals with offering prayers for kings and those in authority (vv. 1-2a). This must have been a disputed issue at the time and may have been a source of dissension in the church's life (v. 8b). The rulers in question were not Christian and they played a significant religious role in the various official cults of the empire. Even so, Paul had already urged the Christians at Rome to obey civil authorities on grounds that all authority is from God (Romans 13:1-5). In 1 Timothy 2:2b, he finds further reason to pray for them: the Christians would be assured of undisturbed, tranquil lives (v. 2b). Paul implies the Christians' prayer would effectively guarantee a better exercise of royal authority over them.

The author finds it necessary to justify these prayers with reasons beyond their immediate motive. God is pleased with them because he is the savior not only of Christians but of all people (v. 3). By praying for non-Christian rulers, Christians gave expression to Christ's universal work of salvation. Indirectly, prayer may also lead rulers to know the truth (vv. 3-6) of which Paul had been made the proclaimer, apostle and teacher (v. 7a). Prayer for civil authorities is thus a special aspect of the mission to the gentiles (v. 7b).

Concluding this development, Paul describes the exterior and interior attitude of Christian prayer. With hands raised and palms facing upward in the traditional suppliant's position, Christians must show a peaceful heart and a blameless life (v. 8).

Luke 16:1-13

In chapter 16, Jesus addresses his disciples directly for the first time since 12:22-53. As background, recall Jesus' words to his host in 14:12-24 and his story of the prodigal son in 15:11-32. In both, Jesus focuses on those who normally should have benefited from his word but did not. In the first passage, they refuse to attend the banquet and the invitation goes to the crowds not originally invited. In the second, the son who stayed with his father refuses to celebrate when his brother returns home repentant.

In today's parable (vv. 1-8), the sinner again enters the gospel. But this time the disciples are told there are lessons to be drawn even from the sinner's behavior. The shrewd, enterprising action of the unjust manager provides a good lesson for those who have become Jesus' disciples. They are not to identify with the manager's lack of justice, but they should learn from the careful way he provided for his future.

The parable provides a point of departure for vv. 9-15, in which earthly goods remain the theme. Wealth is not condemned. However, its insecurity and relative values are emphasized. The wise person uses wealth rightly to secure friends. From the author's point of view, personal relationships in the Christian community are primary, while wealth is secondary (v. 9). Further, the way one uses wealth, in reality a small thing, provides grounds for trusting a person in matters truly great (vv. 10-11). And the way one deals with others' goods leads others to give that same person what is truly his (v. 12). To understand these verses, we must view the gospel as addressing those entrusted with the communal purse destined to care for the community's needy. Their Christian due as disciples will be measured by the way they acquit their responsibility.

Clearly then, when wealth is held in proper perspective it does not in itself stand in opposition to godly matters. But if it did in a particular case, a Christian's service would have been misdirected, and he would be unable to serve God while in the service of money (v. 13).

1. *Amos' courage in denouncing social ills echoes in our times (Amos 8:4-7).*

2. *Our prayer for those who hold civil authority must express our sense of universal Christian mission (1 Timothy 2:1-8).*

3. *Personal and communal wealth must facilitate the development of the Christian and human community (Luke 16:9).*

Twenty-sixth Sunday of the Year

In Christ's kingdom, injustice is righted, and the poor take the place of the rich. Luke addresses those of us who represent the Pharisees, the avaricious people in the Christian community (Luke 16:19-31). Amos' description of Israel's self-indulgent leaders is applicable to us (6:1, 4-7). Paul's word to Timothy should inspire us to live in a manner that leads to life's Christian goal (1 Timothy 6:11-16).

Amos 6:1, 4-7

For the general background of Amos' work, see last Sunday. This reading is from the book's second section (3:1-6:14), which includes three divine pronouncements over the men, the women and the royal house of Israel (3:1-15; 4:1-13; 5:1-6, 8-9) and three woes (5:7, 10-17; 5:18-27; 6:1-14). A woe is like a curse but promises what will take place if the condition against which the woe is spoken is not righted. Like a curse, the counterpart of a blessing, a woe is the opposite of a beatitude.

The third woe is against the leaders of the nation of Israel, who in their complacency and overconfidence betray the people who look to them for leadership (6:1). In 6:4-6, the prophet describes their luxurious, indulgent living: they pursue wanton pleasures with no sensitivity to the collapse of their northern kingdom of Israel. Their behavior and their people's suffering indicate the extent of this collapse, which only needs to be played out in history. They shall be the first to go into exile when Israel is overtaken by her foreign enemies (6:7).

In 6:2-3, omitted from the liturgical reading, Amos draws attention to what has happened to some of Israel's historical neighbors. No better than Calneh, Hamath and Gath of the Philistines, Israel's leaders should take warning from their fate.

Psalm 146:7, 8-9, 9-10

With verses from a hymn of praise, we recognize our responsibility to secure justice for the oppressed in imitation of God who sets captives free (v. 7). Verses 8-9 describe God's generous help, and in v. 10 we proclaim his eternal reign. Together we pray, "Praise the Lord, my soul!"

1 Timothy 6:11-16

Paul has completed his series of instructions to Timothy concerning the roles of various categories of persons in the community (2:1-6:2). He now warns that those who teach otherwise can only be a great source of conflict and trouble (6:3-5a). These people use religion only as a personal means to financial gain (6:5b-10). As a man of God, a classic designation applied to Moses and the prophets, Timothy must flee all this (v. 11a). There follows a short instruction addressed directly to Timothy.

After exhorting Timothy to seek a virtuous life of which several aspects are listed (v. 11b), Paul draws a metaphor from the world of ancient boxing. The active struggle to be virtuous is compared to a fight in the arena (v. 12a). Theologically, life's fight calls for maintaining a firm grasp on the eternal life to which Timothy had been called on becoming a Christian (v. 12b).

In a renewed exhortation, Paul recalls that God gives life to all, and that Timothy's profession of faith had been preceded by Christ's own noble profession before Pontius Pilate (v. 13). With these things in mind, Timothy should be able to remain blameless until Christ's final manifestation (v. 14).

A further statement that Christ's appearance would take place at God's chosen time (v. 15a) indicates that expectations of Christ's imminent return had long faded in the community and that Christians were adjusting to continuing life in the world, an attitude amply attested by this letter's instructions. In the remainder of v. 15 and in v. 16, Paul again cites an early Christian hymn (cf. 1 Timothy 1:17, p. 138).

Luke 16:19-31

Having instructed his disciples on the proper use of wealth (16:1-13), and the Pharisees on the legitimacy of the good news that God's kingdom is open to all (vv. 14-18), Jesus then addresses both groups with the parable of the rich man and poor Lazarus (vv. 19-31).

This parable about wealth and human relationships shows the kind of reversal that takes place in God's kingdom. The rich have no sense of values with regard to money and fail to share generously. They are lost. The worldly poor are saved and made supremely rich. Not that the rich man refused alms, but he failed to extend the kind of hospitality that would have fully nourished the poor. Lazarus had not been offered the table fellowship characteristic of the kingdom (cf. 14:12-24). This parable, which illustrates the sayings found in 16:9-13, is the kind of teaching to which the avaricious Pharisees (v. 14) objected.

However, the story does more than illustrate Jesus' earlier sayings. It also introduces a new element: the futility of signs and authoritative statements to change the behavior of the irresponsible rich (vv. 27-31). If they listened to Moses and the prophets (vv. 29, 31), they would be prepared to hear Jesus' message, spoken in fulfillment of the law and the prophets (vv. 16-17). Since they do not hear, they would not heed the warning even of one raised from the dead. As addressed to the disciples and read in the community of those associated with the risen Lord, the story provides an apologetic for the fact that so many people still cannot hear the teaching of one who has indeed risen from the dead.

1. A prophet like Amos, writing thousands of years ago, still provides us with an examination of conscience (Amos 6:1, 4-7).

2. Like Paul, we should see events in secular life as metaphors for Christian living (1 Timothy 6:10).

3. Faithful behavior springs from faith, not from any proof of a miraculous event (Luke 16:19-31).

Twenty-seventh Sunday of the Year

In today's readings, both Habakkuk and Jesus' disciples face a challenge which appears impossible to grasp. While Timothy's difficulties are not so radical, in context they are no less challenging. None of these persons can avoid this confrontation with reality. Habakkuk must learn to discern between the just Israelite and the unjust nation, Timothy to call on his Spirit-given resources, and the disciples to recognize faith's power.

Habakkuk 1:2-3; 2:2-4

The three chapters of the book of Habakkuk include a titular introduction (1:1) and a dialogue in which the prophet cries out to God (1:2-3; 1:12-2:1). God responds with words of destructive judgment on the unfaithful nation (1:4-11; 2:2-20), but words of life for the just in its midst (2:4). The book ends with a hymn of praise and petition in which the prophet sings of his confidence to God (3:1-19).

The occasion for the prophet's activity was the approach of Nebuchadnezzar's Babylonian armies. This invading force had already destroyed the last refuge of Assyrian power at Carchemish to the north (605 B.C.) and appeared poised to sweep down on Jerusalem (which indeed happened in 597 B.C.). We can understand Habakkuk's desperation before the inevitable (1:2-3). In response, God confirmed Habakkuk's fears (1:4-11).

Renewing his cry, the prophet proceeded to question the rightness of God's ways (1:12-17), while remaining open to further response (2:1). In the Old Testament, Habakkuk emerges as Job's prophetic counterpart.

Equal to the challenge, God reaffirms his general judgment on the nation of Judah but adds that the just, because of their faith, will surely not perish (2:2-20). The liturgical reading takes the initial verses (2:2-4) of this second divine response out of context and associates it with the prophet's initial "Why?" in the face of crisis (1:2-3). In the book of Habakkuk these verses stood as an inspired witness to the fact that God does not condemn the one who questions his ways, if the questioning is part of an open-ended search for understanding.

Psalm 95:1-2, 6-7, 8-9

Psalm 95, a song of praise, provides the dual basis for Israel's exultant response to God, namely, God's relationship to the works of creation (vv. 1-6) and his watchful care in history (v. 7a). The assembly's response, "If today you hear his voice, harden not your hearts," is an adaptation of vv. 7b-8, in which the people are urged not to harden their hearts as in the past at Meribah (Exodus 17:7), when through Moses' intercession God responded to their lack of trust by providing water from the rock (Exodus 17:1-6).

2 Timothy 1:6-8, 13-14

Paul's second letter to Timothy has a community context similar to the first (cf. the Twenty-fourth Sunday of the Year, p. 137). Its message, however, concerns mainly Timothy himself rather than the various categories of Christians in his church. Further, unlike 1 Timothy, it presupposes that Timothy is no longer young (1 Timothy 4:12) but must now see to the transmission of leadership to a new generation (2 Timothy 2:2). As in the case of the Thessalonian and Corinthian correspondence, the two letters represent different stages in a common literary history.

The letter reflects a situation when many have taken a negative attitude toward Paul and his gospel mission (1:15). Whether this must be attributed to the days preceding the end of Paul's life at Rome or to a later situation, as seems probable, it indicates a certain disaffection with the Pauline tradition of Christian life and preaching. This is quite understandable, since in either case the early days of Christianity's planting were long over and the gospel had continued to develop independently of its initial proclamation.

The letter is especially rich in its sensitivity to living tradition. In 1:13-14, Timothy is urged to remain faithful to the way in which Paul himself had incarnated the Christian message (1:9-12). Unfortunately, these last verses have been excluded from the liturgical reading.

In 2:1-2, Timothy is urged to hand on the gospel to others in the same way he had received it from Paul. Earlier in the letter, after a brief thanksgiving and prayer (1:3-5), Paul had urged Timothy to fan the flame of the Spirit-given gift he had received from Paul's hands. This was especially important in the present time of difficulty, when Paul lay in prison and Timothy suffered no small share of hardship as he labored in fidelity to the gospel (1:6-8).

Luke 17:5-10

In Luke 16:19-31, Jesus addressed both disciples and Pharisees. With the beginning of chapter 17, the message is intended for the more limited group of the disciples. It has direct relevance to the internal life of the Christian community.

After two sayings concerning the inevitability of scandal (vv. 1-2), and fraternal correction and forgiveness (vv. 3-4), the apostles ask for an increase of faith to be able to live according to Jesus' teaching (v. 5). They already had faith, but felt unequal to Jesus' challenge. Jesus responded with a hyperbole, indicating that the issue was not one of having more or less faith but of having faith in the first place (v. 6). To shock his apostles into this realization and lead them to reflect on faith's demands, Jesus presents faith's power in terms that stretched physical reality beyond the possible. It is extremely difficult to uproot, transport and transplant a sycamore. It is impossible to plant it in the sea, let alone through a verbal command.

We must view this hyperbole as a metaphor intended to cast light on the author's real concern, which has nothing to do with transplanting trees. Unfortunately, many stop at the image and fail to note it is meant to say something about unlimited forgiveness (vv. 3-4). For the disciples that appeared impossible, but it is possible for those who have faith.

A parable concerning what is expected of the slave (vv. 7-9) is applied to the disciples (v. 10). Jesus' message concerning faith (vv. 5-6) and correction and forgiveness (vv. 3-4) is not an extraordinary requirement to be fulfilled over and above one's Christian commitment. On the contrary, it should be part of the ordinary Christian attitude, for which no reward need be expected beyond that accorded faithful service.

1. *Like Habakkuk, we sometimes cannot grasp the divine wisdom of events in our lives; like him, we must keep our minds open to understanding (Habakkuk 1:2-3; 2:2-4).*

2. *The gift of life received in baptism and channeled in adult life is an undying resource for us as like Timothy we face new challenges (1 Timothy 1:6-8).*

3. *Every Christian is called to extend reconciliation as a normal expression of life in Christ (Luke 17:5-10).*

Twenty-eighth Sunday of the Year

The gospel, summarized in 2 Timothy 2:8-13, must be stead-fastly maintained even in the midst of persecution. It cuts across every territorial boundary and ethnic distinction. Naaman, the Aramean military commander, had been cured by Elisha, an Israelite prophet (2 Kings 5:14 17). Jesus extended healing to Galileans and Samaritans alike (Luke 17:11-19). In today's first and third readings, Naaman and the anonymous Samaritan stand as models of the appropriate response to God's healing presence.

2 Kings 5:14-17

The story of Naaman takes up the whole of 2 Kings 5. He was the commander of the Aramean army, a man highly esteemed by the King of Aram but stricken with leprosy (5:1). In search of a cure, Naaman first goes to the king of Israel at Samaria (vv. 2-7). He is eventually invited to visit Elisha (vv. 8-9), who had succeeded Elijah in the prophetic tradition (1 Kings 2:9-15).

Today's brief segment begins with Naaman's response to the prophet's instruction that he wash seven times in the Jordan (vv. 9-10). The order had appeared too simple (vv. 11-12) but Naaman finally executed it (v. 14) at his servants' urging (v. 13). Cured of leprosy, Naaman returned to Elisha, and the remainder of the reading (vv. 15-17) is taken from their ensuing dialogue (vv. 15-19).

In the presence of Elisha (v. 15a), Naaman confessed his faith in the one
God known and worshiped in Israel, and he offered the prophet a gift (v.
15b). Although Elisha adamantly refused Naaman's gift (v. 16), the latter
nevertheless asked for something in return for what he had offered. His
request for two mule-loads of earth was to provide some Israelite ground
on which he might build an altar and offer sacrifices to the God of Israel in
his native Aram (v. 17). He hoped to circumvent the limitations imposed by
ancient views in which God was considered bound to a territorial kingdom.

Psalm 98:1, 2-3, 3-4

Israel celebrates the victorious salvation which the Lord had manifested
on her behalf in the sight of the surrounding nations. The assembly's
response, "The Lord has revealed to the nations his saving power," situates
the first four verses of this psalm of praise in the Christian context of God's
revelation of saving power to the nations. The responsorial psalm enables
the Christian community to appreciate the story of Naaman as a prefigure-
ment of Jesus' healing encounter with the Samaritan.

2 Timothy 2:8-13

Having exhorted Timothy to maintain the sound teaching on the faith
as he had heard it from Paul (1:13-14; 2:2-3), the apostle recalls the gospel's
core: Jesus Christ, a descendant of David, was raised from the dead (v. 8).
With its emphasis on Jesus' humanity, this summary formulation provided an excellent point of departure for situating the human suffering
that accompanied the gospel's preaching (v. 9). As addressed to Timothy,
Paul's reflections on his own sufferings are intended to be an example of
the staunch attitude called for in one who succeeds Paul in the gospel
ministry (1:13; 2:3).

The apostle may be chained, but there is no chaining God's word (v. 9b).
In spite of limitations imposed on his activities, Paul bears with his
situation in view of the salvation of those whom God has chosen (v. 10) and
whom he now saves through Paul's faithful proclamation of the
unchained word.

Turning to the significance of his own suffering and Timothy's, Paul
draws comfort from his baptism which already expressed a symbolic death
with Christ. This symbolism continues in the life and sufferings of the
baptized. Passing through Christian suffering, the faithful will eventually
live and reign with Christ (vv. 11-12a). In vv. 11b-12, Paul appears to be

quoting an early Christian hymn. Should someone be unfaithful, however, Christ would deny any association with him (vv. 12b-13), and suffering would then lead to death rather than to life.

Luke 17:11-19

For the third time, Samaritans enter the account of Jesus' journey to Jerusalem. In 9:51-56, they serve to bring out the conflict inherent in the mission journey. They show its intended scope transcended Judea and its inhabitants. In 10:30-37, Jesus tells a story that requires his hearers to recognize a Samaritan as their neighbor. He breaks open their accepted classifications of human beings and challenges them to adopt an open attitude towards all.

In today's reading, in an incident situated on the border of Samaria and Galilee, a Samaritan becomes an example of the truly healed person whose gratitude and faith bring salvation (vv. 17-19). As at other points in the gospel, Luke's mention of the journey in this context is intended to counter possible misunderstanding. The journey to Jerusalem in no way implies that Jesus' work is intended only for the Jews.

The Samaritan was one of ten whom Jesus cured of leprosy. We are not told whether all ten were Samaritans. However, in view of the geographical indication in v. 11, and of the emphasis on this foreigner (vv. 16, 18), we may assume the author had a mixed group of Galileans and Samaritans in mind. There are no distinctions in the company of the sick and alienated. Neither should distinctions be drawn among the cured. This is clearly brought out by the fact that the Samaritan, an outcast from a Galilean or Judean point of view, returned to give thanks.

> *1. As in the case of Naaman, God reaches out to us through the simple things around us. To see the extraordinary in the ordinary is the test of faith (2 Kings 5:14-17).*
>
> *2. Baptism was only the beginning of our dying with Christ. Our life as baptized Christians gives meaning to that initial moment as we courageously live the gospel in the midst of the suffering it entails (2 Timothy 2:11-12a).*
>
> *3. The "outsider" in our midst helps us become more sensitive to the simple, sincere attitude that should characterize our response to Christ (Luke 17:11-19).*

Twenty-ninth Sunday of the Year

Today's first and third readings focus on the importance of persistent prayer to God, the source of salvation for all who call on him. Use of scripture for Christian formation, effective because its inspired quality is newly quickened by faith in Christ Jesus, calls for reliance on God as we try to remain faithful (2 Timothy 3:14-4:2).

Exodus 17:8-13

When Moses and the Israelites were finally free from the Egyptians who had pursued them to the Reed Sea (Exodus 14:10-31), they praised God their liberator in song (15:1-21). However, this people still had much to learn about its relationship to the Lord. The stark, barren mountains and expanses of the Sinai provided excellent conditions for discovering the precariousness of life and their radical dependence on God, its continuous source. He provided them with water (15:22-27; 17:1-7) and nourishment (16:1-36). He protected them in their conflicts with desert tribes as they made their way through the Sinai territory (17:8-16). These major theological themes guided the writers of this part of the book of Exodus.

Today's reading recounts Israel's battle with the Amalekites, one of the Sinai's ancient populations. As the first of many battles Israel would fight before settling securely in Canaan, the account teaches them God leads their efforts to victory. This is wonderfully symbolized in the role of Moses, who interceded for his people throughout the battle (vv. 8-13). Verse 14 indicates explicitly the event was to be remembered as a lesson for the future. Israel was very much aware of the tendency to ascribe victory to its efforts rather than to God.

In modern times, when our efforts are sharply focused on maintaining peace, passages like this are difficult to grasp, except perhaps in a theology of liberation. However, we should remember that in Israelite experience, recurrent war appeared to be an inevitable reality and an intrinsic part of the human historical condition. It was quite normal for them to develop a theology of war as in the present reading.

Psalm 121:1-2, 3-4, 5-6, 7-8

Prayerful trust in the Lord, the source of our protection, is this psalm's theme. The assembly's response, "Our help is from the Lord who made heaven and earth," slightly adapted from v. 2, punctuates the expressions of confidence poetically articulated in the psalm's four strophes. The psalm provides an excellent reflection by amplifying the theme of Exodus 17:8-13 and preparing the community for the related themes presented in the other readings.

2 Timothy 3:14-4:2

After reiterating one of 2 Timothy's basic concerns, that Timothy remain faithful to the teaching he had accepted in faith from his teachers (v. 14), the letter discusses the scriptures' role in the work of salvation (vv. 15-17). If v. 15a is an accurate historical recollection, we should conclude that although Timothy was born of a mixed, Jewish-gentile marriage (Acts 16:1), he had been raised a devout Jew, well-formed in the scriptures.

As in other New Testament documents, the term scripture is a reference to the Old Testament, that is, to the law, the prophets and the other books which eventually would be gathered in the collection known as the Writings. Although a number of New Testament books were already at this time gaining universal Christian respect, they were not yet considered part of the scriptures.

Given faith in Jesus Christ, the Old Testament scriptures become a source of Christian wisdom leading to salvation (v. 15). No consideration is given to the value of the scriptures for those who do not share faith in Christ. In v. 16, the practical nature of wisdom becomes obvious. All scripture is useful for teaching, that is, for forming Christians, when its various books are taken up to reprove, correct and train the community in holiness. This teaching through the scriptures effects salvation because it is inspired: it expresses and communicates God's life-giving power. The person taught is prepared to undertake every good work (v. 17).

Timothy had been formed in this manner. Now he must remain constant in forming others in the same way. Paul's charge comes to him at a time when the task runs counter to human convenience and proves a test of patience (4:1-2).

Luke 18:1-8

Although the gospel narrator need not provide each parable with an introduction, Luke usually does in words that identify the story as a parable and attribute it to Jesus. Rarely, however, does this introduction declare the parable's subject. Today's reading is exceptional in that the narrator presents the theme the parable addresses: persistency in prayer.

In Jesus' teaching, the parables were evocative, formative devices open to several interpretations depending on the hearers' personal and social situation. In 18:1-8, Luke directs the readers' attention to that aspect of Jesus' message which in his estimation has become most relevant to their life-context.

Jesus' application of the parable focuses more on the corrupt judge's attitude (vv. 6-8) than on the widow's. Something could be learned from his behavior just as earlier in the gospel Christians had been able to draw a lesson from the shrewd but unjust manager (16:1-13; see p. 141).

The movement of the argument is easy to discern: just as the corrupt judge or the unjust manager, so much more God or the Christian. In 18:1-8, the challenge to Jesus' followers was steadfastness in faith; God would not let them down in times of difficulty.

Luke's interpretation is consistent with this earlier context. But it draws attention away from the judge to the widow who obtained a hearing through her ceaseless importuning. A similar message is found in 11:5-8 as part of a parable commentary on the Lord's Prayer.

The faith (18:8), which must inspire prayer (18:1), is described in 17:5-10 (see p. 146), and the ramifications of the persecution which demands persistence are introduced in 17:22-27.

1. How do the present conditions of urban or rural living lead us to see God's saving presence in our struggle to live (Exodus 17:8-13)?

2. The word of scripture, alive in Christ's followers, effects salvation (2 Timothy 3:15-17).

3. Our prayer must be persistent, trusting and open-ended like that of the widow (Luke 18:1-8).

Thirtieth Sunday of the Year

A person's worth before God is not determined by wealth, education, secular status or official religious position. A good person recognizes his or her humble status in God's presence. This is the main theme of the first (Sirach 35:12-14, 16-18) and third (Luke 18:9-14) readings. The second reading (2 Timothy 4:6-8, 16-18) exemplifies this message from the life of Paul, a highly active apostle who kept his work and person in proper perspective. Paul had had many opportunities to know his poverty. He now knew it as a prisoner for the gospel.

Sirach 35:12-14, 16-18

Both in and out of scripture, the theme of God's justice frequently prefaces considerations on the lot of the poor and underprivileged. However, when Sirach speaks of God's justice, of his having no favorites (35:12), he has both the weak and the strong in mind. Before noting that God hears the cry of the oppressed, the orphan's wail, and the widow's complaint, he states that God is not unduly partial toward the weak (vv. 13-14). This evenhanded approach indicates Sirach must have had a broad personal experience of both the strong and the weak in his world.

God hears the prayers of all who serve him, be they rich or poor (v. 16); but, since the weak are more apt to be in genuine need, Sirach gives greater development to their situation. The prayer of the lowly reaches its heavenly goal and remains there until God responds with justice (vv. 17-18).

This reading provides a good preparation for today's gospel, directed at those who consider themselves God's favorites independently of the way they actually serve him.

Psalm 34:1-2, 15, 17-18, 22

This wisdom psalm emphasizes thanksgiving for God's just response to the needs of the lowly and afflicted. The assembly's response, "The Lord hears the cry of the poor," summarizes the psalm's many elements. Narrower in perspective than the reading from Sirach, the psalm expresses the attitudes of the suffering poor who are truly lowly, that is, who recognize their poverty before God.

2 Timothy 4:6-8, 16-18

Even if 2 Timothy probably stems from a later author and not from Paul, its historical data is very likely accurate. In the form of a farewell statement from Paul, the letter is an important interpretation of Paul's attitude at the end of his life. The author gives a message to his own era in the historical context of the person to whom the discourse is attributed.

In vv. 6-8, the apostle views his death as imminent. Full of confidence, he looks back on the course of his apostolic life and describes it in popular athletic metaphors. Having fought the good fight and won the race, that is, kept the faith, he looks forward to receiving the crown of victory. Similar metaphors earlier in 1 Timothy 6:12 and 2 Timothy 2:5 are consistent with a famous passage in 1 Corinthians 9:24-27 where Paul's concern was primarily with life's contest rather than with victory's reward. From either point of view, it provided an excellent concrete comparison for evoking the striving and the hope which characterize the Christian life.

Verse 16 refers not to Paul's first Roman imprisonment in the early '60s but to a later trial and imprisonment around the year 67. After a long period of house arrest, Paul's first Roman trial had ended in his favor. Following a two-year span of preaching in Rome (Acts 28:30-31), he had been able to leave for the provinces of Asia and Macedonia. There he met further trouble and arrest. He returned to Rome for a second trial. Although the first hearing ended in Paul's favor (vv. 16-17), this was only a temporary stay of execution. Aware of the approaching end, Paul gave glory to God (v. 18).

After the great fire of Rome, when Nero needed to deflect blame from his own unpopular person, Paul, a member of a small group of politically helpless Christians and already a prisoner, proved to be a handy scapegoat. Thus, according to early Christian tradition, Paul won his crown of victory.

Luke 18:9-14

As in 18:1-9 (see p. 151), Luke announces the parable's theme. But this time he carefully identifies those to whom it was addressed, the self-righteous who hold everyone else in contempt (v. 9).

In Jesus' context, the parable contrasted the attitudes of the Pharisee and the tax collector. The setting was Jerusalem's temple. Although the Pharisee seemed to be the just man, his attitude of self-exaltation showed him to be unjustified. His prayer could not be considered genuine prayer.

The tax collector, however, was cut off from the recognized company of the just by his secular position. He was actually justified by his humble attitude before God. Jesus reversed the impressions of religious worth foisted on the people. His view is a specification of the message attributed to John the Baptist in Luke 3:7-9. It was not enough to be offspring of Abraham. One had to reform.

Like our church, the Lukan churches were no longer peopled by Pharisees and tax collectors, and their conflicts had long disappeared. The two, however, had their counterparts in the Christian communities and they retained symbolic value for Luke's addressees. Some Christians had slipped into a pharisaic attitude of self-aggrandizement which labeled others as unacceptable sinners. However, it was not enough to be a distinguished, socially acceptable member of the Christian community. With a traditional saying of Jesus, Luke indicated that the real sinner is whoever exalts. The humble sinner, on the other hand, is the one who is truly exalted in God's eyes (v. 14).

1. God hears the prayer of those who genuinely know their need, independently of their status in life and even of their belonging to the church (Sirach 35:12-14, 16-18; Luke 18:9-14).

2. Paul teaches us to select metaphors from ordinary life to express the nature and ideals of Christian living (2 Timothy 4:6-8, 16-18).

3. Failing to recognize ourselves as sinners, all too easily labeling others as such, we become sinners in God's eyes (Luke 18:9-14).

Thirty-first Sunday of the Year

The universality of God's love and the universal scope of Jesus' offer of salvation are a message of hope which tempers exaggerated emphases on God's punishing justice (Wisdom 11:22-12:1). They counter exclusiveness in the Christian community (Luke 19:1-10). The closely related themes of the first and third readings are supported by Paul's hopeful, pastorally realistic message in 2 Thessalonians 1:11-2:2. Simple in its articulation, the gospel responds to every simplistic avoidance of commitment to life implied in too eager a concentration on the end of time and Christ's return.

Wisdom 11.22-12.1

After calling his readers to a just life (1:1 6:21) and singing wisdom's praises (6:22-11:1; see p. 134), the author demonstrates God's fidelity to his people by means of examples from Israel's exodus experience (11:2-19:22; see p. 123). Five plagues against the Egyptians are contrasted with parallel blessings on Israel.

Today's reading is from a long digression (11:17-12:22) inserted into the author's theological reflections on the way swarms of animals wreaked vengeance on the Egyptians (11:15-16, 23-27; 15:18-16:1) but benefited God's people (16:2-4). The digression concerns God's mercy and was occasioned by the theme of divine punishment (11:16). It tempers the harshness of God's judgment introduced in 11:15-16 and pursued in 12:23

ff. It may consequently represent a somewhat later context than that of the actual account of the plagues.

The meaning emerges clearly when the passage is compared with the account of the plagues. In the latter, we read that God punished the Egyptians through the things they worshipped.

Today's reading exalts God's position as creator (11:22) and affirms his mercy and love for all things (11:23-12:1). Further, God actually ignores people's sins so they may repent. The reason is that, if God hated anything, he would not have created or preserved it in existence. As it is, God loves everything which breathes with his undying spirit. To grasp this last image, recall how man became a living being when God breathed the breath of life into his nostrils (Genesis 2:7).

The passage represents the strongest affirmation of God's universal love in the entire Old Testament. We conclude that the author's situation in Alexandria had become more hopeful than that which called forth the earlier theology of the plagues.

Psalm 145:1-2, 8-9, 10-11, 13-14

A hymn of praise extolling God's royal name (vv. 1-2) and merciful compassion (vv. 8-9) calls all things to give thanks (vv. 10-11) and sings God's faithful care for the struggling and oppressed (vv. 13-14). The assembly's response, "I will praise your name forever, my king and my God," was composed from various elements in vv. 1-2. The psalm provides a good meditative response to the theme of God's universal mercy in the first reading. It also prepares us to appreciate Jesus' gentle but firm offer of salvation in the story of Zacchaeus (Luke 19:1-10).

2 Thessalonians 1:11-2:2

Although the authenticity of 2 Thessalonians is not universally accepted, most arguments against its authenticity have been answered and the modern tendency is to view the letter as genuinely Pauline. Written in early 52 A.D., the letter takes up a number of points 1 Thessalonians had either ignored or treated inadequately. Paul's first letter had been written out of an exuberant sense of gratitude that everything was well with the community at Thessalonica. Paul had been forced to flee that city, leaving the newly established community to cope with the attacks mounted against it as it developed. A positive report from Timothy called forth 1 Thessalonians, with its three chapters of thanksgiving followed by two chapters concerning a number of problems, several of which involved Christ's return on the last day.

In 2 Thessalonians, Paul's thanksgiving and prayer (1:1-12) are far briefer and he turns once again to the question of Christ's second coming (2:1-17). Recalling his earlier teaching while present in Thessalonica (2:5-6) and his first letter (2:14-15), Paul both clarifies and develops his teaching concerning the end of time.

Today's reading includes Paul's summary of his prayer for the community (1:11-12) and the introduction (2:1-2) for his message and exhortation concerning the Lord's coming. Mainly, he warns against groundless agitation concerning that day. Some Thessalonians had concluded from their experience that the day of the Lord was already here. The air was filled with rumors, characteristic utterances and reports of a new letter from Paul. Pleading for calm, Paul asks that all these "sources" of information be ignored as false.

Luke 19:1-10

The tale of Zacchaeus is one of the gems of New Testament storytelling at which Luke excels. Its theme is similar to the parables recounted in 15:1-31 (see p. 138) and 18:9-14 (see p. 154). It differs, however, by presenting the sinner's salvation as the mission of the Son of Man who came to search out and save what was lost (v. 10). The universal scope of this statement, with which the story ends, opens the episode to re-reading in the varied social contexts of Christian history.

The story's introduction (vv. 1-4) sets a lively scene in which various personages are identified and mutually related. In his effort, Zacchaeus is poised between Jesus and the crowd. The body (vv. 5-9) is outlined by an inclusion, the repetition of an important phrase, which in this case sets out the story's basic theme. In v. 5, Jesus says to Zacchaeus: "Today I mean to stay at your house." In v. 9, he says: "Today salvation has come to this house." The substitution of "salvation" for the first person pronoun "I" establishes an equivalency between the two terms, so that Jesus' coming is actually the coming of salvation. Recall that Jesus' name means "The Lord is salvation."

The literary structure of the passage is based on an important play on words through which Jesus' identity and function were revealed. The story concludes with a summary statement concerning the meaning of Jesus' life as Son of Man (v. 10).

1. Around this time of year, many churches celebrate Refor-

158 *The Year of Luke*

mation Sunday. The universalist attitude of Wisdom 11:2-12:1 and Luke 19:1-10 invites us to reflect on the positive contribution of the Reformation to the renewal of church life. But there is the pain of our continuing antagonisms and lack of collaboration in the work of the gospel.

2. An exaggerated focus on Christ's future coming may prevent us from facing our Christian challenge to influence the present course of history (2 Thessalonians 1:11-2:2).

3. Jesus' attitude leads us to set aside our prejudices and to extend his welcoming hand to "outsiders" (Luke 19:1-10).

Thirty-second Sunday of the Year

The first and third readings present the transition between the late Old Testament view of resurrection and Jesus' view interpreted by Luke. The new life of those who have died is God's gift to those who accepted death while living in his service. The second reading sets out the way to new life as God's blessings to be sought in mutual prayer.

2 Maccabees 7:1-2, 9-14

Second Maccabees, an historical book (2:24) named after its principal character, Judas Maccabeus (2:19), is an adaptation (2:31-32) of an earlier five-volume work by Jason of Cyrene (2:23). Covering events from 180 to 161 B.C., its scope coincides in part with 1 Maccabees (175-143 B.C.). Writing late in the second century B.C., the author betrays the influence of Pharisaic thinking, in particular on the question of resurrection (7:9, 11, 14, 23; 14:46).

The author's original purpose was to encourage and edify by retelling the events of the Maccabean war against the Seleucid dynasty of Syria. In its actual form, the book is addressed by the Jews of Jerusalem and Judea to the Jews of Egypt (1:1, 10) as an exhortation to join in celebrating the feast of the temple's purification and dedication (Hanukkah) effected in 164 B.C. (1:9, 18; 2:16).

Today's reading is from one of the three martyrdom accounts in this book (6:18-31; 7:1-42; 14:37-46). The literary style and form of these narratives, the oldest known in their category, strongly marked the many stories written to glorify the heroic last moments of Christian martyrs in the Roman Empire. These accounts, which include the martyrdom of a religiously observant mother and her seven sons (7:1-2), are also one of two pre-Christian biblical indications of growing belief in God's resurrection of the just. The other source is Daniel 12:2-3, 13.

In 2 Maccabees, resurrection, a divine gift of endless life (v. 9), applies only to the just. The unjust are punished by being deprived of this life (v. 14). This theology, strongly related to biblical reflections on retribution, emphasizes the positive (reward) rather than the negative (punishment) aspects of divine justice. This emphasis would also characterize the New Testament, where we frequently find no concern with what happens to the unjust at death. Christian resurrection, after all, is a share in the new life of Jesus whom God raised from the dead.

Psalm 17:1, 4-6, 8-15

The prayerful lament of a person unjustly accused (Psalm 17) provides a fitting meditative reflection on the lesson from 2 Maccabees. Bringing his case to Yahweh (v. 1) and affirming his innocence (v. 4b), the psalmist pleads for a divine response (v. 6) and protective love. He confesses his confidence that he will once again be at peace in God's presence (v. 15). The assembly's response, "Lord, when your glory appears, my joy will be full," allows us to apply the psalm to the hope of new life after the crisis of death.

2 Thessalonians 2:16-3:5

Paul had introduced his message on the Lord's second coming (2:1-12) with a warm expression of thanksgiving and prayer (1:3-12). He now concludes on the same tone (2:13-17) but in a manner which already introduces the exhortation that follows (3:1-15). Today's reading is from that second thanksgiving passage and from the first part of the exhortation.

Chapter 2:16-17 is a prayerful blessing similar to those which conclude most of Paul's statements of gratitude; it has a parallel in 3:5. Having asked that God console their hearts and strengthen them for every good work and word (2:16-17), he later requests that God rule their hearts in his love and in Christ's constancy (3:5).

Paul addresses the Thessalonians as his brothers (3:1a), an important designation indicative of the common bond that joins those who share God's life in Christ. As in the gospel tradition, Christian relationships transcend family ties. The apostle asks that his brothers pray for him and his co-workers, Silvanus and Timothy (1:1), that the Lord's word may continue to spread (3:1b). He views his gospel message as God's word. The Thessalonians had received it that way (1 Thessalonians 2:13). They are also asked to pray that he be delivered from confused and evil people who have no faith (3:2). Their prayer is grounded in God's faithfulness. He will guard them from evil (3:3) and keep them faithful to Paul's teaching (3:4).

Luke 20:27-38

Chapters 20 and 21 of Luke's gospel present Jesus' teaching in the Jerusalem temple (20:1; 21:37-38) during his mission's last days before his farewell banquet and the passion-resurrection. Addressing the high priests, the Pharisees and the elders (20:1-8) or the people in their hearing (20:9-19), he also dealt with emissaries (20:20-26) and the Sadducees (20:27-38), who tried to trap him to no avail through questioning on subtle issues (20:39-40).

Today's reading is the episode with the Sadducees, an especially tricky test. In the name of the law of Moses, the doctrinally conservative Sadducees did not subscribe to more recent views of resurrection or any affirmation of immortal life for the individual person (v. 27). In the hearing of the scribes, most of whom were Pharisees who did maintain God would raise the just to life on the last day, they presented Jesus with what they considered an insoluble problem (vv. 28-33). If the risen life included marital relationships, would not the very notion of resurrection be self-contradicting?

Avoiding the trap, Jesus replies first by denying their fundamental assumption. Marriage is not an issue for those who are God's offspring in the resurrection. The risen life transcends marriage (vv. 34-36). Second, Jesus appeals to traditional language to which the Sadducees themselves subscribed. Doesn't Moses speak of the Lord as the God of Abraham, Isaac and Jacob? And is God not a God of living? They must consequently admit the patriarchs are living and there is a resurrection of the just (vv. 37-38).

In Jesus' argument the patriarchs already are risen and living. This differs from the Pharisees who associated the resurrection with the future end of time. In the concluding statement, Luke has Jesus sidestep imaginative representations of the resurrection by speaking of the living rather than the risen (v. 38b). He avoids popular tendencies to reduce the resurrection to the resuscitation of a corpse. The passage prepares us to understand the nature of Jesus' resurrection as presented in Luke 24.

> 1. *New life after death, like our present life of faith, must be viewed as the creator's gift of hope calling for commitment to his service (2 Maccabees 7:1-2, 9-14).*
>
> 2. *The more outstanding one is in apostolic dedication, the*

more one should be aware of human fragility and the need for prayer and God's gift (2 Thessalonians 2:16-3:5).

3. Resurrection is a term applied to the new life of all who live in God's presence (Luke 20:37-38). Consequently we can speak of all who have died in Christ as already risen from the dead. This attitude should influence our view of death and its celebration in a funeral liturgy.

Thirty-third Sunday of the Year

Straining beyond the difficulties and the persecutions at hand, Malachi and Luke look forward to a day when all will be righted in the balance of God's justice. This does not mean, however, that present sufferings are meaningless. As historical manifestations of God's purifying presence for those who remain steadfast in the way of the law and the gospel, they prepare the post-exilic Israelites and Christ's followers for the Lord's definitive advent. In 2 Thessalonians, Paul draws attention to the living gospel incarnate in his attitudes and behavior. The imitation of Paul and of those who truly heard his word provides God's word with human immediacy for all who courageously respond to the challenge of Christian living.

Malachi 3:19-20

The prophetic activity of Malachi, a proper name created from the expression "my messenger" (1:1; 3:1), was directed to the population of Judah some 75 years after Israel's liberation from Babylon (538 B.C.). Gone was the intial enthusiasm of the return and retoration, gone the exuberant hope of Haggai and Zechariah (520 B.C.). The situation confronting Malachi was disillusionment, stagnation and bitter questioning of God's ways (1:2, 6-7; 2:17). Why serve him (3:14 15)? The prophet's response prepared the way for the reforms soon to be undertaken by Ezra and Nehemiah in the second half of the fifth century B.C.

After denouncing the priests, the levites and the people for their attitudes and behavior (1:2-2:17), the prophet announces the advent of a divine messenger who would prepare the day of the Lord's coming (3:1-24). The function of the messenger, identified with Elijah the prophet (3:23), would be to purify the people, refining them with fire just as gold and silver are refined (3:2-3).

Today's short reading contrasts the lot of the proud and evildoers (v. 19) with those who fear God's name (v. 20) when his messenger comes. Those who truly revere God as he manifests himself will emerge free and happy for the Lord's coming, while those who refuse to recognize their dependence on God will be utterly destroyed. For the former, purifying fire will act like the sun's healing rays. The latter, on the other hand, will be destroyed like wood which, unlike gold and silver, is reduced to ashes by the flames.

Psalm 98:5-6, 7-8, 9

On the Twenty-eighth Sunday of the Year, the liturgy prayed with Psalm 98:1-4. Today's meditation hymn is from the remaining verses of this psalm of praise. Orchestra and choir are called to praise the Lord as king (vv. 5-6). Seen through the community's appreciative faith, the sea and the earth and all the life that fills them, even the rivers and the mountains are ordered to do the same (vv. 7-8) at the approach of creation's ruler (v. 9). The assembly's response, "The Lord comes to rule the earth with justice," a proclamation based on v. 9, is a one-line summary of Malachi's prophetic work.

2 Thessalonians 3:7-12

The imitation of Paul (3:7a), an exhortation found in all the apostle's letters, is an extremely important aspect of his message. In Jesus' mission and in early Christian teaching and preaching, no less than in the earlier Jewish tradition, the proclamation of God's word was not merely a matter of words but of interpersonal communication. The gospel was carried and expressed by the apostle's life, much like the law or Torah was interpreted and transmitted by the life of faithful Jews. Interiorized in a concrete human person, the gospel word was an articulation of a graced life with Christ. To receive the gospel is consequently not so much a matter of hearing the word as of responding to a person.

In 3:7b-12, Paul applies this basic principle of imitation (v. 9b) to the particular problems at Thessalonica. There was unruly behavior occasioned by aimless activity tantamount to idleness. Some community members obviously were taking advantage of the generous sharing policy. Whether this attitude was connected with the view that the day of the Lord and the messianic banquet were already fully manifest (2:2) is not clear. This view, however, could easily have led to the passivity attacked by Paul.

In response, Paul points to his own behavior at Thessalonica, where he worked for his livelihood, providing an example of Christian responsibility. Indeed he had even laid down the rule, now recalled, that those who refuse to work should be barred from the community table (v. 10). In our times, we should take care not to apply this principle to the socially deprived. Paul assumed that work was available to all. In our industrial culture, that is often not the case.

Luke 21:5-19

Chapter 21:5-36 of Luke's gospel includes many elements of Mark's account of the apocalyptic consummation of creation and history (Mark 13). In Luke, however, the significance of events is judged quite differently. For Mark the events affecting Christians at the destruction of Jerusalem and the temple constitute the beginning of the end. Luke is very careful to state that, although these things will come to pass, the end is not yet. Persecution and internal strife are part of the church's history on earth; but the end once thought imminent will come only when the entire course of the church's mission is fulfilled among the gentiles. Luke disassociates Jerusalem's destruction from the end of time.

Intermediate events are seen as part of Luke's theology of persecution. In retrospect, they mark new stages in the church's developing mission by providentially moving the gospel proclamation out of the narrow circle in which it tends to become entrenched. Christians must not be misled by false claims of Jesus' return (vv. 7-8). Rather they must endure difficult times courageously that through them they might be saved (v. 19).

The one-verse introduction for vv. 5-19 is also indicative of Luke's interpretation and application of tradition. In Mark 13:1, the solidity and the enormity of the temple and its building blocks occasion Jesus' discourse; in Luke 21:5 it is the temple's rich adornment with precious stones and votive offerings. The author considers these of no real value. Just as the two copper coins of a poor widow are worth more than the offerings of the rich (21:1-4), so is the community's simple but genuinely personal worship worth more than the magnificence of a temple which now survives only in human memory and in the debris of its destruction.

> *1. Christians are challenged to respond to the discourage-ment of those who would abandon the new law in difficult times. Their response must be energetic and alive with Christ's hope; it must also be realistic, viewing sufferings and problems in the context of religious purification (Malachi 3:19-20).*
>
> *2. Like Paul we should live a life worthy of imitation. Faith*

*and other Christian attitudes are shared not by teaching their
definition but by concretely revealing their credibility and their
human value (2 Thessalonians 3:7-12).*

    *3. Worship's value is determined by the genuineness of the
community's life-offering, not by the glory of its external manifestation (Luke 21:5).*

Thirty-fourth Sunday of the Year (Christ the King)

*Our celebration of Christ's kingship, radically unlike that of
earthly rulers, is introduced by a reading from 2 Samuel, in
which a pastoral image tempers the power of David's ruling
office. David's kingly rule had united disparate tribes with a
natural tendency to consolidate in distinct kingdoms. Transcending Old Testament perspectives, Luke shows how Jesus
the Christ assumed royal power by surrendering human glory
to the point of giving his life on the cross. In the Colossians'
reading, Paul sets out the attitudes of those who accept the
Father's dominion, the basis of life in his Son's kingdom.*

2 Samuel 5:1-3

    The two books of Samuel narrate the creation of the Davidic royal
dynasty in Israel. Originally one work, later divided into two scrolls, the
books are named after the prophet who was instrumental in transforming
the various territories governed by judges into a united kingdom. In their
final form, as part of a history which included the two books of Kings, the
books of Samuel affirmed Israel's historical roots for a people which had
just seen the final collapse of the southern kingdom of Judah (2 Kings 25).

    While still a youth, David had been anointed by Samuel to be the future
king of Israel (1 Samuel 16:1-3). This promise was fulfilled in two stages.
First, David was anointed by the elders of the southern territories to be the
king of Judah (2 Samuel 2:1-7). Second, the elders of the north anointed
him king of Israel (2 Samuel 5:1-5). Both anointings took place while
David was still at Hebron before the capture of his capital city, the mountain stronghold of Jerusalem (2 Samuel 6:6-12) from whose central position he would rule both Judah and Israel. In this we recognize the hand of

writers who organized independent traditions to affirm the religious hegemony of Jerusalem over the whole land of promise.

The basis of the northern kingdom's union with the south is given in 5:1, where the tribes of the north proclaim their tribal, ethnic unity with David's family. On the basis of David's past exploits (5:2a), however, he was singled out (5:3) to shepherd the Lord's people and be Israel's commander (5:2b). These two aspects of David's office, shepherding and military leadership, complement one another and indicate ideally how his power should be exercised with pastoral gentleness.

Psalm 122:1-2, 3-4, 4-5

The first five verses of this song of Zion proclaim the joy of going to Jerusalem, the seat of God's dwelling (v. 1) and of his royal government through the house of David (v. 5). The psalmist sings of Jerusalem's beauty (v. 3) as the place for giving thanks to the Lord's name (v. 4). The response, "I rejoiced when I heard them say: let us go to the house of the Lord," is a slight modification of v. 1, placing emphasis on the exhortation as actually heard by the community rather than as addressed to it.

Colossians 1:12-20

For the background to 1:15-20, which may be Paul's adaptation of an early Christian hymn, see p. 114.

Romans and Colossians are letters to communities not personally evangelized by Paul. Paul had never even visited Colossae (1:4; 2:1). The origins of the community at Rome were very likely due to Romans returning from pilgrimage to Jerusalem. The Colossian church had been established by Epaphras, a Colossian (4:12) who had been one of Paul's associates at Ephesus (1:7). He was with Paul at the time of the letter's writing (4:12).

Not knowing the Colossians from his own experience, Paul shows himself less personal than in other letters. However, his willingness to write indicates a growing sense of responsibility among the churches for one another's well-being as well as Paul's ability to love even those he did not know but who shared his Christian values. The letter is an important witness to the church's growing awareness of its universality, directly attested to in 4:14-16.

In 1:12-14, we have the concluding section of Paul's prayer thanksgiving for the Colossian community's progress. In fulfillment of Paul's prayer, the Colossians should give thanks to the Father who has made them worthy to join the saints in light (v. 12). In this, we sense a word of indirect admonition and subtle correction. The Colossians may have viewed their being out of darkness (v. 13a) and in the light as the fruit of their own efforts rather than of God's fatherly sharing of his life by bringing them into his beloved Son's kingdom (v. 13b). Through the Son our sins have been forgiven and we have been redeemed (v. 14). Paul affirms his Christian solidarity with the Colossians and recognizes their development in the Spirit (1:6, 8), but he refers to the Spirit in language meant to realign them with the gospel truth (1:5).

Luke 23:35-43

The Lukan passion narrative is rich in the theology of Christ's kingship. In God's kingdom (22:16, 18), which is also Jesus' kingdom (22:30) assigned to those who continue his work in history (22:29), the apostles are not to act like earthly kings (22:25). Later, in the trial scene, Jesus rejects Pilate's understanding of the kingly title. Only the term is similar (23:3). In Jesus' mind, God's reign and the dominion he had received (22:29) had nothing to do with Roman political lordship.

Today's reading points to the irony of the inscription fixed to the cross: "This is the King of the Jews" (22:38). Jesus was indeed king but his assumption of kingship reversed current notions of royal power. Giving life to the full, he saved his life and ours not by seeking it but by losing it (9:24; 17:33). Unwittingly, in mocking tones, the leaders of the people (v. 35), the soldiers (v. 37) and one of the criminals crucified with Jesus (v. 39) articulated the salvific meaning of Jesus' dying on the cross.

> 1. *Leadership roles in the church, varied as they are, are all assumed through the church's recognition of demonstrated ability to lead (2 Samuel 5:1-3).*
>
> 2. *Church leaders must transcend the narrow horizons of those in their pastoral care and reach out to others in a gesture of solidarity and concern (Colossians 1:12-20).*
>
> 3. *Church leaders exercise their role in God's kingdom by giving themselves to the full. Leading the community to assume a like attitude, they build up the church's unity and contribute to a fuller manifestation of God's reign (Luke 23:35-43).*

Movable Feasts and Solemnities

168

Holy Trinity

Christianity's sacramental nature is grounded in the Trinity. God (= the Father) manifests (= the Son) and effectively communicates (= the Spirit) his life in human history. John 16:12-15 presents this mystery with a focus on the Spirit's relationship to Jesus the risen Lord. Creation reveals God's eternal wisdom (Proverbs 8:22-31), and Christian love gives human expression to God's act of loving (Romans 5:1-5). They are the ultimate context, the concrete experiential locus of God's sacramental manifestation.

Proverbs 8:22-31

The introductory portion of the book of Proverbs (chapters 1-9) is a long instruction on the value of wisdom for both young and old (1:4). At two points in this long development, a personification of wisdom speaks out in the first person. The lyrical tone contrasts with the didactic poetry which characterizes the ordinary language of the teacher of wisdom.

Today's reading sings of wisdom's privileged position at the world's creation (vv. 22-31). It provides the most fundamental reason why all should be attentive to her (8:1-11, 12-21). Verses 22-26 affirm God's creation of wisdom before all else was created. Recalling Genesis' first chapter, wisdom evokes various aspects of the physical universe, the depths, the springs, the mountains and hills, the earth and its fields and even the very first dust of the earth. She proclaims she was brought forth before all these.

In vv. 27-31, wisdom announces her presence at the creation of all things, the heavens, the skies, the fountains of the deep, the seas and the foundations of the earth. This second poetic list refers to aspects of the universe even more fundamental than those in vv. 24-26. Present at creation, wisdom was God's master workman, rejoicing in his presence and his world, delighting in the human beings who inhabited it. The human race and the created universe are manifestations of God's wisdom, reflections of the creator who made them. This theology prepared the way for Christian sacramental reflection in which visible created realities are signs of the invisible and divine. By contemplating the universe as a created expression of its creator, we share in the biblical writer's vision of wisdom.

Psalm 8:3-4, 5-6, 7-8

God's glory is manifested in all creation, especially in the human person. His name or manifestation is truly majestic. The hymn contrasts our humble status (vv. 3-4) with our extraordinary dignity (vv. 5-8). Both are presented in relation to the rest of creation. In our contemplation of the heavens, we appear to be nothing (vv. 3-4). However, God has given us dominion over all the works of his hands (vv. 5-8). This paradox calls for our proclamation of God's majestic name.

Romans 5:1-5

In Roman's "doctrinal" portion (1:16-11:36), Paul carefully sets out his position on several basic issues confronting the early church. Justification and salvation are the fundamental themes of Romans, indeed of much of Paul's preaching. Romans 5:1-5 introduces the letter's second part and recapitulates his teaching on justification presented in 1:16-4:25. Along with 5:6-8, these verses provide a transition to the second part (5:1-11:36) whose theme is salvation.

Romans 5:1-5 is an excellent example of Pauline experiential theology, quite different from the biblical or historical theology developed in Romans 4 and 9-11. To follow Paul, the reader must verify the apostle's statements in his or her own experience. Writing in the first person plural, Paul associates the reader's experience with his own. He enables us to organize various aspects of Christian experience and to perceive their interrelationships. The theological force of this development lies in the reader's ability to confirm each step in the argument from experience and to see the inner connection between the various steps.

The elements to be verified are, first, that we boast of our hope and even of our afflictions (v. 3a). At this point, Paul's intention may be more hortatory than indicative. This attitude must be firmly grounded. Hence the second step which presents afflictions as the source of endurance (v. 3b), endurance as source of tested virtue, and tested virtue as the ground of hope (v. 4). The argument's experiential nature is underlined by Paul's "we know that . . . " (v. 3b). The ultimate criterion, however, which concludes the argument, affirms that the ground of hope is Christian love, the human expression of God's act of loving (v. 5).

John 16:12-15

Jesus' announcement of the Spirit's coming, an event associated with the manifestation of the risen Lord, presents the Spirit's role in relation to Jesus and the Father. Although Jesus would have far more to tell his disciples, they are not yet in a position to understand his message (v. 12). Later, however, the Spirit of truth will illuminate them. At that time, he will announce things received from Jesus (vv. 13-14), which Jesus himself received from the Father (v. 15).

This portion of Jesus' farewell statement is significant for its elaboration of trinitarian relationships. The Father is the ultimate source of revelation; Jesus, its transmitter, but only for a time. After his death, the Spirit is the direct source of revelation and Jesus its intermediate source. After Easter, revelation is a process from the Father to the Son, from the latter to the Spirit, and finally from the Spirit to the faithful disciples.

John 16:12-15 is also important for understanding the theological methodology of gospel narratives. Since all that the Spirit later inspires has its source in Jesus, it was possible to attribute all later developments of faith understanding to the historical Jesus. Thus the gospels could credit Jesus with teaching which in fact reveals a long process of faith experience and development in the Christian community.

> 1. *The created universe is a visible manifestation of God's creative personal being. Sensitivity to the world around us should consequently facilitate our gradual introduction into God's life (Proverbs 8:22-31).*
>
> 2. *The presence of God's life in us can be verified from the quality of our love for others, the living manifestation of God's own love (Romans 5:1-5).*
>
> 3. *Theologically grounded in the relationship of the Spirit to Christ and Christ to the Father (John 16:12-15), revelation is perceived through the visible universe (Proverbs 8:22-31) and God's historical presence in Christian love (Romans 5:1-5).*

Corpus Christi

*In the eucharist we are challenged to nourish others as Jesus
had nourished his disciples (Luke 9:11-17). This is made possible by the risen Lord's active presence in the community which
gathers for a memorial of him (1 Corinthians 11:23-26), prefigured in Melchizedek's festive hospitality to Abraham (Genesis
14:18-20).*

Genesis 14:18-20

The brief account of Abraham's meeting with Melchizedek (14:18-20)
was inserted into the story of the patriarch's return from victory over four
Mesopotamian rulers (14:17-24). As we read in v. 18, Melchizedek, whose
name means "Zedek is my king," was king of Salem. The text is uncertain,
however, and could read "a king allied to him," that is, to Abraham.
Melchizedek was also a priest of the God Most High (El-Elyon), a Canaanite name for God whom the Israelites identified with Yahweh the God
of Israel (14:22).

As king, Melchizedek extended hospitality to Abraham and provided
him with nourishment. "Bread and wine," that is, food and drink, refer to a
full festive meal. Since other food was taken with bread, it was the most
significant part of the meal. All food could thus be designated by the
simple term bread. Since water was served with ordinary meals, the mention of wine indicates the meal's festive nature. In context, the meal was
appropriate for Abraham's victory celebration.

As priest, Melchizedek pronounced a blessing on Abraham (vv. 19-20a),
praying that Abraham be blessed by God Most High and that God himself
be blessed. In the blessing's first part, God is presented as creator of heaven
and earth. The second part emphasizes God's continuing role in history. In
return for Melchizedek's hospitality and blessing, Abraham gave him a
tenth of the possessions recovered in battle.

Although the text did not originally refer to the eucharist, its use on
Corpus Christi helps us appreciate the eucharist as a festive celebration, an
expression of worship and a call for divine blessing. In the present context,
the eucharist is seen as the work of the creator who continues to lead and
protect his people through history.

Psalm 110:1, 2, 3, 4

A royal psalm celebrates Jesus' enthronement as king and priest. The
king shares in God's lordship, and God establishes his dominion over all

his enemies. The footstool refers to the ancient practice of inscribing the names of conquered peoples on the royal dais (v. 1). The king rules from Zion or Jerusalem, which is the symbol both of his particular kingdom and of his relationship to other nations (v. 2). All will acknowledge the king's position over them (v. 3), and this divinely given position is firmly established forever (v. 4).

1 Corinthians 11:23-26

From an historical point of view, this passage is one of the most important in the New Testament. Through its introduction (v. 23a), which resembles 1 Corinthians 15:3a (see p. 97), an early liturgical formula for the eucharist can be traced as far back as the early '40s when Paul was being apostolically formed as a leader of the church at Antioch.

The formula's passion setting for the eucharist would later influence the gospel writers and result in the narrative presentation of the eucharist as a last supper in which Jesus bade his disciples farewell. Luke's account of the last supper would include the same liturgical text as formulated at a later stage in the life of the Antioch community.

The eucharistic action is described in short succinct phrases: Jesus took bread, gave thanks and broke the bread (vv. 23b-24a). After the supper he took the cup (v. 25). In turn, both actions were interpreted by Jesus as being his body for the disciples, that is, the self-offering of his person, and the new covenant in his blood, that is, his life which established a new set of relationships among the participants and with God.

In relation to his body or person, Jesus asks that in remembrance of him the Christians make his act of self-giving their own. In the bread and the cup of his life, Jesus presents the eucharist as a proclamation of his death, that is, of his ultimate act of self-giving. He indicates its relationship to the fulfillment of history with the Lord's coming. The same attitude toward the future was articulated in the succinct liturgical prayer: "Come, Lord Jesus" (1 Corinthians 16:22; Revelations 22:7, 17, 20; see also p. 82).

Luke 9:11-17

Luke's account of the feeding of the 5,000 is an early narrative tradition concerning the eucharist's origins in the historical life of Jesus. It differs from the Last Supper account by situating the eucharist outside the context of Jesus' passion. By including it in his gospel, Luke presented the story as a stage in the institution of the eucharist, later supplemented by the Last

Supper and the post-resurrection meal celebrated with the risen Lord at Emmaus.

The narrative emphasizes the disciples' role in leading the crowd and serving Christ's bread. The disciples had bread in an extremely limited quantity. Shared at Christ's command, it proved to be an abundant nourishment, more than sufficient for all. The eucharist fulfilled God's word that there would be much left over (cf. 2 Kings 4:42-44). In their early efforts to grasp the eucharist's significance, the Christians saw themselves as sharing in the abundance provided by Jesus.

Unlike Mark's account, the setting for the multiplication is the city where Christians lived in communities and gathered at the home of prominent members. The number of baskets filled with what was left over corresponds to the number of apostles. The multiplication is related to the eucharist of the apostolic church over which the Twelve would preside.

> *1. The eucharist is a festive celebration marked by a spirit of hospitality as well as an expression of worship and a prayer for God's blessing on ourselves and our endeavors (Genesis 14:18-20).*
>
> *2. The quality of our eucharist is determined by the manner in which we carry out Christ's command to make his act of self-giving our own. In this way the participants give visible expression to the sign of Christ's love (1 Corinthians 11:23-26).*
>
> *3. By sharing what we have, however modest, ordinary nourishment becomes the sacrament of that abundant, satisfying banquet God offers through Christ (Luke 9:11-17).*

The following solemnities and feasts replace the Sunday when their dates fall on the first day of the week.

February 2
Presentation of the Lord

The Lord's Presentation is a celebration of hopes fulfilled, both for Jesus and those who greeted him in Jerusalem and for us. Those hopes involve breaking through social boundaries and reaching out universally (Luke 2:22-40). This Christian mission brings struggle and purification (Malachi 3:1-4). Our fear of suffering and death is its most basic hindrance (Hebrews 2:14-18).

Malachi 3:1-4

The reading includes two distinct units. In the first, God makes a solemn pronouncement, in the first person singular, about his messenger (3:1). The second presents the questioning, reflection and response provoked by God's word (3:2-4). We cannot tell whether the second unit concerns the messenger's work or God himself. Since the messenger is God's agent, the author may have deliberately obscured the distinction between them.

God assures Israel he is sending his messenger. The Hebrew for "my messenger," *malachi*, is the source of the name given the book's otherwise anonymous author. Tradition saw the book itself as the promised messenger. In 4:5, the messenger is identified with Elijah, a role fulfilled in the New Testament by John the Baptist. The person sent is a messenger of the covenant, God's relationship and presence to his people. He prepares the people for the Lord's coming. The Lord is introduced as the object of the people's search, and his covenant as their desire (3:1).

The response (3:2-4) focuses on the day of the Lord and the difficulty in coping with this divine manifestation. After two introductory questions, the difficulty is explained. The divine presence is like a fire that refines gold or like lye that purifies wool. Those called to offer sacrifice will be purified, so that what they offer in the people's name will once again please the Lord.

Psalm 24:7, 8, 9, 10

Our response is from a liturgical dialogue. Inside the temple, a hymn has been sung (vv. 1-6). At the gate, we await entry (vv. 7-10). We are returning in procession with the ark of the covenant, bearing the symbols of divine presence. The assembly interrupts the leader's prayer and moves him to greater insistency: "Who is this king of glory? It is the Lord!"

Hebrews 2:14-18

This reading emphasizes the limitations of human beings, Jesus' relationship to those limitations, and the purpose of his coming.

We are human beings, flesh and blood, not angels. We struggle with temptation and are enslaved particularly by our fear of death. Jesus, truly incarnate, shared fully in our humanity. He too was tempted, but he was never enslaved by fear of death. He accepted this most radical limitation of humanity.

The result was his victory over the prince of death whose stranglehold on humanity he broke. He affirmed human freedom for himself and for us. As our brother who suffered with us, he became our mediator and intercessor before God. Fulfilling the creator's intentions for humanity, our high priest helps us who by temptation fall short of God's design for us.

Luke 2:22-40

Luke's infancy narrative concludes with two visits to Jerusalem (2:22-40 and 41-52). The first (today's reading) is Jesus' presentation to the Lord. It focuses on Jesus' significance in light of his origins. The second draws attention to his significance in terms of his ultimate destiny with God.

The reading begins with the journey to Jerusalem (2:22-24) and ends with the return to Nazareth (2:39). The text emphasizes Jesus' careful fulfillment of the law. The concluding summary (2:40) describes Jesus' gracious development, flowing from the law's fulfillment. Reference to wisdom prepares us for its manifestation (2:46-47) during the second visit when Jesus was 12 years old (2:42).

Between the journey's two phases (2:22-24, 39), Luke introduces two figures, Simeon (2:25-35) and Anna (2:36-38). They represent Israel's living expectation and prophetic voice. Through them, Israel witnesses to God's fulfillment, in Jesus' person, of his promise to expand revelation to all peoples. Jesus' universal salvation was precisely in fulfillment of the law and Israel's intended role in history. The universal mission was not a rejection of Israel. By inaugurating this mission, Jesus would truly be the glory of God's people. In 2:34-35, Simeon alludes to the suffering that will accompany this opening of salvation to all peoples.

1. We yearn for the Lord's coming into our lives, but are we prepared for the purification it implies (Malachi 3:1-4)?

2. To live in true freedom, we must accept death's eventuality. This is the message of Jesus' life (Hebrews 2:14-18).

3. Today's feast invites us to examine our participation in Jesus' universal mission and to rededicate ourselves to its realization (Luke 2:22-40).

June 24
Birth of John the Baptist

John the Baptist is the biblical prototype for one aspect of Christian life: expectation and promise. Like him, from the womb we have been called to prepare the Lord's way (Luke 1:57-66, 80). With him, our prophetic word leaves the past behind and looks to future salvation (Acts 13:22-26). In him, we find the model of God's servant, called to speak his word, eager to proclaim his glory (Isaiah 49:1-6).

Isaiah 49:1-6

The liturgy applies to John the Baptist a song of God's servant (Isaiah 49:1-6). The New Testament sees Jesus in these songs; but in Isaiah, they refer to the prophet who embodies Israel's experience.

Called from the womb and named by the Lord, the prophet recognizes the source of his vocation and mission (v. 1). The song describes the effectiveness of the prophet's word: a sharp sword in God's hand, a polished arrow hidden in his quiver (v. 2).

God will be glorified through his servant (v. 3), but this is not obvious to the prophet. He feels he has labored in vain (v. 4). God reassures him. He formed the prophet from the womb to be his servant. God will be his strength in the task of gathering Israel (v. 5). The mission is extensive: it reaches to the gentiles, to the ends of the earth (v. 6).

Psalm 139:1-3, 13-14, 14-15

God sees into the deepest self; nothing remains hidden from him (vv. 1-3). He knows us because he created us (v. 13). We celebrate life by acclaiming the wonder of his current deeds (v. 14), reflected in the mystery of our origins (v. 15). The assembly praises God's creativity experienced in its life: "I praise you for I am wonderfully made."

Acts 13:22-26

Paul accepts an invitation to address the synagogue at Antioch in Pisidia (13:13-15). In his review of Israel's history, he ends with God's choice of David as king (v. 22) and introduces David's descendant, Jesus, as Israel's savior (v. 23). At this point, Paul refers to John the Baptist and his mission (vv. 24-26).

True to his gospel presentation of John, Luke describes him as a herald or proclaimer rather than a baptizer. Luke draws attention to his prophetic role in the framework of a general theology of promise and fulfillment (v. 24). He mentions baptism as the object of John's call for repentance.

As in the gospel, Luke separates John's mission from that of Jesus. When his career is ending, John rejects false notions about his identity and subordinates himself to Jesus (v. 25). After this citation, Paul declares John's salvific message was given "to us." That "us" includes Paul, his companions and his audience, i.e. children of Abraham and all who reverence God. John's work and message are valid for the gentile mission as well as for the original mission to Israel.

Luke 1:57-66, 80

Each gospel writer considered John the Baptist an extremely important figure. He set the historical stage for Jesus' role in the drama of biblical history. Only Luke, however, relates Jesus and his work to John's birth. Looking back to the origins, Luke tells the birth story with its implications for John's mission and his relationship to Jesus.

The extraordinary birth called for rejoicing, because once again the Old Testament was fruitful (1:57-58). At the baby's naming, everyone expected the child to receive his father's name, Zechariah (v. 59), reinforcing the continuity of Old Testament history. But the parents call him John. The new name indicates his unique role in history. He is a transitional figure (vv. 60-63). Zechariah has finally believed (cf. 1:18-22), and his faith allows him to utter God's praises (v. 64).

The event causes wonder and fear of the Lord throughout Judea. John's identity is a question. He is obviously more than merely the son of Zechariah and Elizabeth (vv. 65-66). After Zechariah's canticle (vv. 67-79, omitted by the *Lectionary*), the narrator gives a simple summary of John's growth (v. 80). Luke juxtaposes the extraordinary and the ordinary to show God's marvelous signs at work in the lives of believers open to God's self-manifestation.

> 1. *Like John, we have been called, formed and named from the womb to be the Lord's servants in a mission to all the world (Isaiah 49:1-6).*

> 2. *John proclaims "to us" that Christ will come through us to enrich our lives (Acts 13:22-26).*

3. Our lives are like John's: full of promise, pointing to God's definitive manifestation in Christ, expecting his coming in glory. John helps us understand our place in history: Christ is present, but not fully (Luke 1:57-66, 80).

June 29
Peter and Paul

We honor today the apostle to the Jews and the apostle to the gentiles. Their extraordinary roles flowed from their experience of Christ and their public profession of faith. In Matthew 16:13-19, Simon Peter speaks for himself and for all who stand on the church's rock foundation. For both Peter (Acts 12:1-11) and Paul (2 Timothy 4:6-8, 17-18), the apostolic role involved suffering with Christ, the risen Lord and savior.

Acts 12:1-11

Persecution is an important concern in Acts. The people for whom the book was written were actually experiencing various forms of persecution, leading many to hesitate about their Christian faith. In today's first reading, Luke presents Herod's persecution of Peter in a manner that evokes Jesus passion. He also shows how Peter was liberated. As with Jesus, his persecutors' hopes were frustrated. Luke wants his readers to come to a faith understanding of their persecutions and to look to the future with trust and hope.

Like Jesus, Peter is arrested during the Feast of Unleavened Bread and his trial must wait until after Passover. However, he is freed during the night of the feast. Passover proved to be Jesus' time of liberation, too.

Peter's story is told in vivid detail: the double chains, the guards, the angel of the Lord. Luke draws us into the tale. The iron gate opens of itself, and Peter thinks he is dreaming. Once free, he recovers his senses. Throughout, we listen closely with excitement and feel like applauding at the end! Luke achieves his purpose by lightening the community's discouragement. The story is true, because it is *our* story.

Psalm 34:2-3, 4-5, 6-7, 8-9

The community punctuates this hymn of divine praise with a proclamation of the Lord's protection. Pledging to bless God forever, the psalmist invites the humble to rejoice (vv. 1-2). They are to proclaim God's greatness as they join him in a liberating search for a God (vv. 3-4) who helps those who turn to him (vv. 5-6). Those who find shelter in the Lord are happy and safe in his presence (vv. 7-8).

2 Timothy 4:6-8, 17-18

Cf. second reading, Thirtieth Sunday of the Year, pp. 153-154.

Matthew 16:13-19

The question of Jesus' identity, that is, his religious significance in history, is frequently raised in the gospel literature. The disciples, of course, knew him as Jesus, the name that singularly expressed his personal being, but this did not exclude the need to interpret the meaning of that person. Hence the many titles attributed to Jesus: "the prophet," "the Son of Man," "the Son of David," "the Son of God," and others.

In Matthew 16:13, Jesus inquires concerning people's grasp of who the Son of Man is. The answer moves away from titles to the names of historic personages in Israel's history. Jesus would embody the religious significance and function of people like John the Baptist, Elijah, Jeremiah or one of the other prophets (v. 14). Jesus then addresses the disciples' own belief, and Simon Peter answers that he is the messiah, that is, the Christ, God's anointed, and the Son of the living God (vv. 15-16). He responds with singular titles that distinguish Jesus from any other person and proclaim his royal salvific role as well as his expression of God's life. As Jesus states, this understanding can only come from his heavenly Father (v. 17).

Addressed as blest, Simon is then declared the rock foundation of a church unassailable by death (v. 18). This ecclesiastical perspective is unique in the synoptic gospels, a significant departure from Matthew's source in Mark 8:29. Peter's historic ecclesiological function is further defined in the following verse, where Jesus promises him the keys of the kingdom (v. 19a). His position is an authoritative one; it allows for binding and loosing, terms associated with the function of Jewish rabbis in matters of life and belief (v. 19b). The passage clearly indicates the Matthean community's recognition of Peter's authority in the foundational stage of church history.

   1. Like Peter, every Christian follows Christ's way from suffering to liberation (Acts 12:1-11).

2. Paul teaches us to select metaphors from ordinary life to express the nature and ideals of Christian living (2 Timothy 4:6-8, 17-18).

3. Like the Matthean community, we affirm the continuity of our Christian life and faith with that of Simon Peter, the rock on which the church is firmly founded (Matthew 16:13-19).

August 6
Transfiguration

The transfiguration of the historical Jesus shows us the meaning of his life in light of his future resurrection (Matthew 17:1-9) as an expression of faithful, worshiping humanity in God's person (Daniel 7:9-10, 13-14). In 2 Peter 1:16-19, that transfiguration scene stands with prophetic announcement and authenticates the message of Peter who had been one of its witnesses. Witness to the transfiguration is equivalent to witness to the resurrection.

Daniel 7:9-10, 13-14

Apocalyptic literature, like the book of Daniel, includes vivid descriptions of visions in which the author strains at the limits of language to express his experience of God's transcendence. Today's reading includes two passages from a vision. One presents God himself (7:9-10); the other, a mysterious figure compared to a son of man (vv. 13-14). In both, take careful note of the symbols and examine what is said through them.

God, the Ancient One, is enthroned. His appearance is brilliantly white (v. 9a), a characteristic of divine manifestations, for example, in Jesus' transfiguration. The reference to wheels (v. 9b) evokes the vision of Ezekiel 1, where the throne is on the chariot bearing the ark of the covenant. The scene is a cultic one: in v. 10b, thousands and hundreds of thousands attend the Ancient One. The fire (vv. 9b-10a) is symbolic of the divine judgment executed in vv. 11-12.

The next scene describes a second transcendent figure, one like a son of man, that is, a human being. When he presents himself to the Ancient One (v. 13), he receives dominion, glory and kingship which is doubly universal (v. 14). First, his dominion extends not to Israel alone but to all nations; and second, it is everlasting, unlimited by any period of time.

The "one like a son of man" is a personification and an idealization, a representative of Israel, glorious in God's presence, an Israel firmly established, unthreatened by the foreign nations actually in its service. The figure is a powerful symbol of Israel's hopes, needed at a time when the foreign forces of Hellenistic Syria were invading Israel both religiously and politically. Many Israelites adopted foreign ways, eroding Israel from the inside. The same expression, son of man, would later become one of Jesus' most significant titles.

Psalm 97:1-2, 5-6, 9

Verses 1-2 and 5-6 describe a theophany in language characteristic of divine manifestations in both Testaments. Verse 9 is a statement of praise exalting God as the Most High, dominating all the earth. The community sings in response: "The Lord is king, the most high over all the earth."

2 Peter 1:16-19

The second letter attributed to Peter is very likely the latest work in the New Testament. Dating from about 125 A.D., it has many parallels with the earlier letter of Jude and is aware not only that Paul's letters have been collected but that some of the apostle's statements have become controversial (3:15-16). The letter's major concern is the non-fulfillment of Christian expectations regarding Christ's second coming (3:1-13).

To authenticate his teaching, the writer appeals first to his experience of Jesus' sovereign majesty (1:16-18). The ample description leaves no doubt that the transfiguration is the event in question, and we must conclude the author was aware of the gospel narrative tradition concerning Jesus.

The transfiguration is presented as a genuine experience of eyewitnesses, quite different from the concocted myths the readers might have heard. Emphasis, however, is not on the vision itself but on the divine word, "This is my beloved Son, on whom my favor rests."

In 1:19a, the prophetic message found in the scriptures (v. 20) is a second authenticating factor. The readers are exhorted to focus on the prophets, tiny lamps in a dark place. Eventually the dawn will come to dispel their interior darkness. While rejecting idle speculation on the time of Christ's return, the author retains a sense of Christian tension between life's present moment and its definitive goal.

Matthew 17:1-9

The transfiguration enters the gospel immediately after Jesus' first prediction of the passion-resurrection (16:21-23) and his call for discipleship as a joining in the way of the cross (16:24-28). It is part of the gospel's view of Christian life in history. It presents the meaning of the cross as a passage to glory both for Jesus and those who follow him. As v. 9 indicates, the transfiguration's significance will become clear only with the Son of Man's rising from the dead.

With Jesus already in glory, the passage becomes a sign of our future association with him in that glory (v. 4). Desire for glory, however, is not fulfilled before the Christian way of the cross is completed. The account also indicates how Jesus was manifested as God's beloved Son by his rising and how the fulfullment of his life manifested him as Israel's divine teacher (v. 5b). Finally, the experience occasioned reflection on Jewish and early Christian hope for Elijah's return (vv. 10-13). The disciples were made to realize that Elijah already had returned in the person of John the Baptist (v. 13).

Moses and Elijah, who appear in the scene, may be symbolic of the law and the prophets. But far more important is their evocation of traditions that they would return at history's final moment. If John the Baptist is Elijah already returned, is Jesus then not the new Moses at the dawn of a new, definitive covenant?

> *1. Israel's vision of itself as "one like a son of man" provides an ideal symbol for the Christian community's call to enter into God's presence and to assume its responsibility in manifesting God's dominion on earth (Daniel 7:13-14).*
>
> *2. Like the early Christians, we ponder our experience of Christ as well as the scriptures in our search for understanding the history unfolding about us (2 Peter 1:16-19).*
>
> *3. For those who share Jesus' vision and join in his mission, the promise of glory is already manifested in his resurrection (Matthew 17:1-9).*

August 15
Assumption

Christian life comes to full flower in the woman who gave life to salvation. Mary's visit to her pregnant cousin and her song of praise become our visit and our song (Luke 1:39-56). Revelation's vision of the woman describes our historical situation and the promised victory (Revelation 11:19; 12:1-6, 10). Paul shows how we too share in Christ's resurrection (1 Corinthians 15:20-26). Today, Mary is a prophetic sign for our future.

Revelation 11:19; 12:1-6, 10

An ancient Near Eastern myth describes an evil monster's pursuit of a goddess about to bear a savior-king. Under divine protection, the child is born and grows up to slay the monster. Elements of this myth are applied to Christ and the church in their struggle against evil (12:1-6). The conflict is clothed in the language of God's biblical manifestations (11:19).

The woman symbolizes both the old and the new Israel. As the ideal people of the old covenant, she is shown in the sky, surrounded by creation's luminous bodies. The 12 stars represent Israel's 12 tribes and prefigure the 12 apostles, the new Israel's heads (12:1). In labor, the woman is the old Israel, straining toward fulfillment in the person of the messiah (12:2). As her labor proceeds, evil's formidable forces arise in the heavens to destroy her child (12:3-4).

Evil fails. The boy lives to become the powerful leader, not only of Israel but of all nations. He eventually ascends to God's throne (12:5). Contrary to the pagan myth, evil is not yet destroyed. The woman, now the new Israel, must flee to the desert, a place of formation and purification where God cares for her (12:6). The author is aware of historical stages in biblical history. He understands the church's meaning: with its origins in Israel, the church continues on earth after Christ's exaltation until evil's final defeat.

Psalm 45:10, 11, 12, 16

This nuptial ode praises the bride and the bridegroom—a fitting psalm to celebrate Mary's union with God. The community's response adapts v. 10: "The queen stands at your right hand, arrayed in gold."

1 Corinthians 15:20-26

In vv. 1-11, Paul has presented the tradition concerning Christ's resurrection. He reveals the Corinthians' inconsistency in rejecting the resurrection of Christians (vv. 12-19). In vv. 20-28, Paul reaffirms Christ's resurrection. Today's reading omits the last two verses of this third unit.

The metaphorical expression, "firstfruits," is based on the ancient Israelite thought that the firstfruits represented symbolically the entire harvest. As the "firstfruits of those who have fallen asleep," Jesus' resurrection is the initial expression of the resurrection that will include all those who are in Christ (v. 20). Paul describes Christ's role as parallel to Adam's. In Adam all died; in Christ all will come to life again (vv. 21-22). Through our identification with Adam, we tend toward death. By our new identification with Christ, we pass through death to life.

The resurrection is part of an historical schema that explains creation's consummation. First, there was Christ's resurrection. At his coming, his followers' resurrection will occur (v. 23). Then the end will come. Having vanquished death and established his reign, Christ will hand the kingdom over to the Father (vv. 24-26). This schema is Paul's effort to develop a new synthesis for understanding the end of time. He incorporates Christian belief and experience into a Jewish apocalyptic model.

Luke 1:39-56

After Elizabeth's greeting, Mary responds to her kinswoman with a beautiful canticle, the *Magnificat*. Verse 56 summarizes the remainder of Mary's visit.

Mary's thanksgiving song is a mosaic of Old Testament references. The most prominent source is Hannah's song in 1 Samuel 2:1-10. Like Hannah, Mary praises God for her child. The conception is God's mighty act on her behalf. The author has in mind not just the conception but the entire life work of the child born to Mary.

The opening statement proclaims Mary's joyful response to God (vv. 46b-47). Of the canticle's three stanzas, the first emphasizes the work of a mighty, merciful God on his lowly servant's behalf (vv. 48-50). The second shows how God's acts reverse ordinary expectations about those who are humanly mighty and lowly, hungry and rich. These are God's ways in salvation history (vv. 51-53). The last stanza interprets the event as God's mindful mercy toward his servant Israel. The servant theology developed in the Old Testament proved extremely important for New Testament christology. The canticle implies that Mary is Israel: in her, God fulfills the enduring promise made to Abraham and his descendants (vv. 54-55).

1. The church's life is formation and purification. Protected by God after Christ's salvific victory, the church struggles with evil as she moves toward life's fullness with God (Revelation 12:1-6).

2. For Christ's followers who live in him, the resurrection of Jesus as the Christ is a clear sign of hope for life eternal (1 Corinthians 15:20-26).

3. Through Mary's acceptance of a role in salvation's story, God fulfills the promise of Israel's history. We are heirs to that promise, grateful to Mary but challenged by her attitude (Luke 1:39-56).

September 14
Triumph of the Cross

The cross is the symbol of Jesus' exaltation. For believers, his ignominious death is the source of eternal life (John 3:13-17). The book of Numbers recalls Moses' bronze serpent (21:4-9), a symbol John used to illustrate the significance of Jesus' death. With the hymn of Philippians 2:6-11, we explore the mystery of human life which gave meaning to Jesus' death.

Numbers 21:4-9

The scriptures were not written in a cultural vacuum. For instance, many of Canaan's religious institutions, practices and symbols contributed to the Israelites' formulation of their special faith experience. One of these symbols, a bronze serpent, plays an important role in this reading. Archeology and ancient literature show us serpents as significant elements in Canaan. The serpent, an agent of death, is held up as a source of protection and life. This phenomenon is also found in other religions of Asia.

The people rebel and grumble against God and Moses over the difficulties encountered in the exodus. God sends serpents to punish them with death. In repentance, the people turn to God and pray for life. God orders a bronze serpent raised aloft. Those bitten recovered when they turned to the image. Like Christ's cross (John 3:13-17), the source of death becomes the source of life.

Psalm 78:1-2, 34-35, 36-37, 38

In 72 verses, Psalm 78 tells how God dealt with Israel and how the people responded with ingratitude. The verses of our meditative prayer include the psalmist's appeal for a hearing. He wants to recall events that are an authoritative part of tradition (vv. 1-2). He reveals the people's fickleness and describes their deceitful expressions of love (vv. 34-38). Together we sing, "Do not forget the works of the Lord!"

Philippians 2:6-11

Cf. second reading, Passion (Palm) Sunday, p. 56.

John 3:13-17

Nicodemus asked how a person can be begotten by the Spirit (3:9). Jesus testifies to the source of his knowledge (3:10-12). Verse 13 recalls the gospel's prologue: the Word in God's presence (1:1), the Word come down from heaven to empower with divine sonship those who accept him (1:12), the Son revealing the Father (1:18). Even as he tells the story of the Word made flesh (1:14), John presents Jesus at his Father's side (1:18) in heaven (3:13). The risen, exalted Lord speaks through the historical Jesus.

The passage compares the lifting of Jesus and Moses' raising of the bronze serpent (see first reading). The reference, of course, is to Jesus' death on the cross, to bring eternal life to believers (vv. 14-15). This was God's purpose in giving his Son. Acting out of love, God had no intention to condemn the world but to save it through his Son (vv. 16-17). The subsequent verses show how condemnation comes only to those who reject the Son and refuse to believe. For them, the cross does not fulfill God's loving purpose (v. 18-21).

The challenge John issues goes to the heart of Christianity. Concretely, it is not easy to see the cross as a sign of God's love. However, those who accept Christ's life are led gradually to accept its implications.

> 1. *When we rebel against freedom, we bring death upon ourselves. Like the Israelites, we are saved by death's symbol. For us, it is Christ's cross (Numbers 21:4-9).*

> 2. *Jesus' absolute acceptance of the human condition (including death) resulted in God's exalting him to new life (Philippians 2:6-11).*

> 3. *As the symbol of Christ's selfless love, the cross expresses the triumph of his life and death (John 3:13-17).*

November 1
All Saints

All three readings contrast our present historical state as Christians with the state of heavenly blessedness which awaits us if we are faithful in God's service and in Christian fellowship, even under pressure of difficulties and persecution. Celebrating all those who have reached the fullness of salvation, among whom we include our deceased relatives and friends, we focus on our own hope of salvation and the fundamental attitudes required for its attainment.

Revelation 7:2-4, 9-14

Two visions describing the heavenly church (7:1-8; 9-17) have been inserted between the breaking open of the first six seals (6:1-17) and the seventh seal (8:1), symbols of the various stages in the coming of the day of the Lord. The purpose of these visions is to contrast the glory of the saved, at worship before the throne of the Lamb, with the panic-stricken inhabitants of earth at the opening of the sixth seal (6:12-17). In 6:17, the author asked: "Who can withstand it?" The answer is given in the visions which provide today's reading.

After the sixth seal is broken, the universe as seen through the human eye is in panic (6:12-17); the heretofore unrelenting movement toward the end is halted, as divine messengers check the forces of nature (the four winds) and halt all destruction of living things (7:1, 2b-3a). This is to allow the angelic symbol of life and divine protection to approach from the East, the region of Paradise (Genesis 2:8), and to seal the foreheads of God's servants with the sign of divine ownership (vv. 2a, 3b-4). Those marked will be protected by God just as an earthly ruler looks after everything which bears his seal.

In vv. 9-17, the author describes the heavenly liturgy of those marked with God's seal who have survived the day of vengeance. The vast assembly of the saved (vv. 9, 13-14a) praises God and the Lamb, the risen Lord through whose sacrifice they had been made clean (v. 14b), as the source of salvation (v. 10). The heavenly court (v. 11) responds with an extensive doxology (v. 12). The hymnic conclusion (vv. 15-17) of the second vision is not included in today's reading.

Psalm 24:1-2, 3-4, 5-6

The responsorial verses are taken from the first two strophes (vv. 1-6) of one of Israel's processional psalms (vv. 1-10). After singing God's creative dominion over creation (vv. 1-2), the psalmist inquires who can stand before God in his holy place (v. 3). Liturgically, this question and the answer (vv. 4-6) echo the salvation theme from the book of Revelation. The assembly's response, "Lord, this is the people that longs to see your face," is appropriately based on v. 6, applying the psalm and Revelation 7:9-14 to the eucharistic gathering.

1 John 3:1-3

The first letter of John, written sometime between 90 and 100 A.D., emanates from the same community and writer or writers responsible for the final stage in the development of John's gospel. Its emphasis on the humanity of Jesus as a "sacramental" communication of God's word (1:1-2) is already well known from the gospel's prologue (1:14, 18).

The letter's basic message concerns the meaning of Christian life. This is also true of the gospel; but in keeping with the tradition of gospel narrative, we have there a presentation of Christian life through the person and mission of Jesus. The letter deals directly with the life of Christians who share the life of the Son and give historical expression to God's personal presence and love.

These themes underlie today's brief reading, which opens with a word of contemplative gratitude for the new life of Christians as children of God. The new "nature" enjoyed by Christians is rooted in God's fatherhood. The bond between Father and children is God's creative love which initiated the relationship and maintains it in existence (3:1a). This the Christians recognize, although the world, that is, sin and all that is opposed to the light (1 John 1:5-7; John 1:4-12), does not. The reason is that it did not recognize the Son, through whose fellowship we are God's children (3:1b).

This is the present state of Christians. What we shall be later when we enter into that life's fullness, we do not know because it has not yet been revealed. What we do know is that we shall be like God and see him as he is (v. 2). The reading concludes with an indirect exhortation to living a holy life founded on what awaits us in hope (v. 3).

Matthew 5:1-12

The initial verses of today's reading introduce the first of five major discourses intimately related to the fundamental structure of Matthew's gospel (chapters 5-7; 9:35-11:1; 13:1-53; 18:1-19:1; 24:1-26:1). The conclusion of this discourse, popularly called the sermon on the mount, is given in 7:28-29. A comparison with a much shorter parallel discourse which Luke situates on a plain (6:17-7:1) shows that the author's purpose was to present a synthesis of Jesus' teaching given in various places and on multiple occasions. The mountain setting is theological rather than historical. Like Israel's great lawgiver on Sinai, Jesus, the new Moses, presents the new law from the mountain.

The remainder of the reading presents Matthew's version of the beatitudes (vv. 3-12), which combines an earlier tradition outlined by an inclusion, "The reign of God is theirs" (vv. 3, 10), and a literary expansion by the gospel's author (vv. 11-12).

The earlier version of the beatitudes (vv. 3-10) with its sharply defined parallelism and inclusion stands close to oral tradition. Contrasting the present state of Jesus' followers as poor in spirit and persecuted for holiness' sake with their future blessings in the fullness of God's reign (vv. 3, 10), it specifies their blessings as consolation for the sorrowing, inheritance of the land (the new Israel) for the lowly, fullness for those who are now hungry and thirsty, God's merciful love for those who show mercy, the vision of God for the single-hearted, and sonship of God for the peacemakers (vv. 4-9).

The last of the traditional Matthean beatitudes, which concerns persecution (v. 10), provided the writer with an opportunity to add a beatitude regarding persecution for the sake of Christ. Different in style and addressed directly to the readers ("Blest are *you*"), the addition was called for by the persecution of the Jewish Christian community, recently excluded from rabbinical Judaism as organized during the decades which followed the destruction of Jerusalem in 70 A.D.

> 1. *Those who serve God in recognition of their relationship to him are God's people, protected from ultimate destruction (Revelation 7:2-4, 9-14).*
>
> 2. *Sharing in Jesus' sonship, we live in hope for the full manifestation of life with God, a life which we cannot define except in relation to what we already enjoy (1 John 3:1-3).*
>
> 3. *Even in the midst of a difficult situation (Matthew 5:3-6, 11-12), we are truly blest so long as we reach out to others with the human manifestation of God's reign which we even now possess (Matthew 5:7-10).*

December 8
Immaculate Conception

Today's solemnity celebrates the goodness of human life. Mary was an individual human person, but she is a living symbol of salvation. Created by God, we take our place in the universe as personal signs of his presence. With Mary we are called to accept our creaturehood and to reach out to the creative source of goodness. The promise spoken in Genesis 3:9-15, 20 takes flesh in the fiat of Luke 1:26-38. In Ephesians 1:3-6, 11-12, we sing our gratitude to God who has gifted us.

Genesis 3:9-15, 20

From the 10th century B.C., an ancient author reflects on the basic evil of every human being (Genesis 3:1-24). The key to the passage is the serpent's temptation, "You will be like gods" (v. 5). The story is well-known: human beings find it difficult to accept the human condition. Straining after divinity and refusing the status of co-creator, Adam causes his own destruction and ultimate death.

Today's reading begins after the sin of everyman as God searches him out. Stripped of dignity, the man hides (vv. 9-10), and eludes responsibility by placing blame on the woman (vv. 11-12) who in turn blames the serpent. In the ancient Near East the serpent was a symbol of ruse and deceit. It also represented immortality by annual "rebirth" through the shedding of its skin. Condemned by God, the serpent will be crushed by the woman's offspring (vv. 14-15). Liturgically, this hopeful message complements the sin and finds completion in Mary, who is the new Eve, "the mother of all the living" (v. 20).

Psalm 98:1, 2-3, 3-4

This psalm of praise is a fitting meditation on today's solemnity. Luke echoes the poetic language in the hymns of his prologue, especially the *Magnificat*. We joyfully recognize God's marvels on our behalf and respond with exuberant gratitude. The community's response, "Sing to the Lord a new song, for he has done marvelous deeds," is from Psalm 98:1 and punctuates the psalmist's review of the reasons for this joyful outburst.

Ephesians 1:3-6, 11-12

Two segments of a hymn of praise (1:3-14) introduce Paul's message for the Christians of Ephesus. The two sections focus on God's predestination of the Christian community to their present state of life in Christ.

The Christian community appears in the first person plural—we, us, our. What is true of all Christians, namely that God acted on their behalf before the world began (v. 4), was surely true of the woman selected as his Son's mother. Chosen by God, all Christians are called to be holy, blameless in God's sight, and full of love (v. 4).

Luke 1:26-38

Part one of Luke's infancy narrative opens with the announcement of the Baptist's birth (1:5-25) and concludes with Mary's visit to Elizabeth (1:39-45). Between the two episodes, the author presents a second announcement story, concerning the birth of Jesus, and Mary's acceptance to be his mother (1:26-38). When Mary visits Elizabeth (v. 26), she is pregnant with Jesus. In context, the author shows the superiority of the one who "will be called the Son of the Most High" (v. 32) over the man whose function would be to "prepare for the Lord a people well-disposed" (1:17).

By stressing Mary's virginity (vv. 27, 34), Luke emphasizes Jesus' transcendent origins: his life cannot be understood in the limited terms of human history and physical generation. Correlatively, Mary's role cannot be understood in purely biological terms. God was with her (1:28). She realized the ideal of the covenant relationship whereby God was present to his people Israel.

She is the human point of the divinity's insertion into human life (vv. 30-33). She became the Lord's servant (v. 38), that is, a humble human being whom God made a major turning point in Israel's history. She was open to God's transcendent action.

1. *Our Christian challenge is to refuse to ratify "original sin" in our lives; like Mary, we must withstand any tendency to reject our created humanity (Genesis 3:5).*

2. *As with Mary (Luke 1:28), God's providence prepared each of us for our mission in life (Ephesians 1:4).*

3. *Mary's openness to God's word is the ideal expression of the Christian attitude (Luke 1:38).*

Hear Father Eugene LaVerdiere
on NCR Cassettes

In addition to his written works, Father Eugene LaVerdiere has recorded for NCR Cassettes a number of programs and talks on scriptural subjects. These cassettes may be ordered from NCR Cassettes, P.O. Box 281, Kansas City, Missouri 64141.

The Gospel of St. Luke

Prominent scripture scholar Eugene LaVerdiere presents this commentary on Luke, the gospel in which he specializes. Use this program for a deeper study of the texts proclaimed in the liturgical year of Luke. *Twelve cassettes (24/20-minute segments) with printed study guide in vinyl shelf album. (A-977-A-988)* **$79.95**

Acts of the Apostles

No study of Luke is complete without his second volume, the Acts of the Apostles. LaVerdiere, a well known expert on Luke, applies his skills to this written history of the early church. *Twelve cassettes (8 hours) with study guide in vinyl shelf album. (A-989-A-1000)* **$79.95**

Paul the Proclaimer

Everyone *talks* about evangelization. This program is about a person who evangelized. By exploring Paul's message and method, LaVerdiere shows that Paul is the proclaimer for our times. He also covers the topics of God's love, God's word, the Christian community, Christian roles (especially of women), the risen Lord, Christology, the eucharist. *Five cassettes (4 hours) in vinyl album. (A-637-A-641)* **$39.95**

Suffering to Glory

LaVerdiere looks at Christianity's most sacred traditions— Jesus' death and resurrection. He examines the New Testament texts and shows we share the challenge of the early Christians: to recognize the presence of the risen Lord in our lives. *Two cassettes (2 1/2 hours) in vinyl album. (A-429-A-430)* **$19.95**

The New Testament Servant

LaVerdiere examines the spirituality of Christian ministry in the synoptic gospels and applies it to today's ministers. Both early and modern ministry share the same problems and joys. *Five cassettes (over 5 hours) in vinyl shelf album. (A-1094-A-1098)* **$39.95**

At the Table of the Lord

What did the eucharist mean to the early Christians? LaVerdiere finds an answer in the many eucharistic references in the New Testament. *Seven cassettes (5 hours) in vinyl album. (A-777-A-783)* **$49.95**

Presidency of the Assembly

LaVerdiere discusses the emergence of leadership roles in the eucharistic assembly during the first century. *One cassette (44 minutes). (A-529)* **$7.95**

An Exegete Looks at the Lectionary

How does revelation take place in the liturgy? LaVerdiere

Order from NCR Cassettes, P.O. Box 281, Kansas City, MO 64141.

shows how the lectionary gives us a new gospel for our day. *One cassette (58 minutes). (A-629)* **$7.95**

Seasons of the Liturgical Year
LaVerdiere teams up with liturgist John Gallen, S.J., to show how you can enrich liturgical celebrations throughout the year. *One cassette (75 minutes). (A-669)* **$8.95**

Praying with the Scriptures
Here's how to turn scripture reading into meaningful prayer. LaVerdiere believes that, to pray scripture, you must understand its meaning in relation to your life, while sharing the attitudes behind all scripture—faith, hope and charity. *One cassette (67 minutes). (A-670)* **$8.95**

The Word of God Revealed and Made Flesh
LaVerdiere examines those scripture texts that speak of the imitation of Jesus. He shows how we can be God's word to each other. *One cassette (42 minutes). (A-667)* **$7.95**

Reflecting the Gospel
Your challenge in reflecting the gospel, says LaVerdiere, is to present the word in new ways. Just as Jesus and his message were interwoven in the word, your person is communicated with the message you speak. *One cassette (50 minutes). (A-741)* **$7.95**

One Church, Many Gifts
LaVerdiere shows how we are one church, one body in Christ, guided by the Spirit. *One cassette (59 minutes). (A-748)* **$7.95**

The Kingdom is You

God's kingdom is not just for the future. LaVerdiere proves the kingdom is a model for Christian life today. *One cassette (43 minutes). (A-750)* **$7.95**

New Testament Ministry for Today

LaVerdiere helps you examine your ministry in this powerful study of early New Testament communities. *One cassette (46 minutes). (A-857)* **$7.95**